INVESTING:
MORE SUCCESS, less stress
with
TrendPoint!

Wayne Grennan, PhD

Timberlea Press

Copyright 2002 by Wayne Grennan

No part of this book may be reproduced or transmitted in any form or by any means, electronic or mechanical, including photocopying and recording, or by any information storage or retrieval system without written permission from the author, except for brief passages quoted in a review.

National Library of Canada Cataloguing in Publication

Grennan, Wayne, 1938-
   Investing : more success with less stress / Wayne Grennan.

Includes bibliographical references and index.
ISBN 0-9730848-0-4
     1. Investments. 2. Stocks. I. Title.

HG4521.G74 2002   332.63'22   2002-901935-4

Published and distributed by:

Timberlea Press

18 Hillside Drive,
Timberlea, NS
B3T 1H2
Canada

Email: info@timberleapress.com

Website: www.timberleapress.com

Cover artwork by Nancy Roberts

Website design by Deborah Keema

PREFACE

This book has come into existence as a result of my decision to manage my own pension fund in a Life Income Fund context when I retire. It was also motivated by a professional interest in how reasoning is done in the investment field. (My academic research specialty is argumentation and logic.) Subsequently, I have found that I agree with Jonathan Steinberg's opinion that "hunting for great stocks is endlessly stimulating and challenging. It is an intellectual process full of nuance. Reasoning skills are constantly tested, and analytical assumptions must be shaped and reshaped against a perpetually changing backdrop."

Not having had formal training in finance and investment theory, I think I have been able to look at stock investing without the preconceptions (prejudices?) that one acquires from academics in these fields. Because of this, you are apt to find the contents of this work rather critical, especially about the buy-and-hold philosophy preached by most professional investment advisors. On the other hand, investing theory is very quantitative, if done right, and I do have the requisite mathematics background acquired in an "earlier life" as an engineer. But despite the need by the author for some statistical skills for doing a project like this, the reader will be able to appreciate the force of the statistical evidence frequently deployed without anything more than a knowledge of arithmetic.

You will benefit more from the material presented here if you have a bit of personal stock buying experience and have read a bit on how stock markets work. I will also assume that you are computer-literate enough to be able to use investment websites such as "quote.yahoo.com" or "globeinvestor.com". These days all the information you need to make investment decisions is available on the web. And most of it is free!

Wayne Grennan Ph.D.

CONTENTS

Chapter One: Investment Choices, Conventional "Wisdom"

Investment Instruments 2
Bonds 2
Stocks 3
The Stock-Bond Portfolio 5
The All-Fund Portfolio 7
Summary 8
Guerrilla Investing? 8
The TrendPoint! Strategy In Outline 10
The "Old-Time Religion": Buy and Hold 12
Can The Markets Be Timed? 14
The Trading Ineptness Of The Amateur 16
Prohibitive Trading Costs? 17
The Nortel Example Again 18
Conclusion 20

Chapter Two: Selling

Selling By Target Price 22
A Stop-Loss Strategy 23
Playing With House Money 23
A Selling Strategy 24
Psychological Impediments To Successful Selling 35

Chapter Three: Selection and Purchase of Stocks

Introduction 41
The Universe Of Stocks 44
Dangerous Sectors 46
Evaluation Parameters 51
Price/Earnings Ratio: P/E 52
Forward P/E 53
P/E To Earnings Growth (PEG) 57
Price To Sales Ratio: P/S 60

Momentum Measures 63
Valuing Stocks 64
Price/Earnings Ratio..64
PEG Ratio 68
P/S Ratio 70
Momentum 70
TrendPoint! As A Buy Strategy 72
Selecting Large-Cap And Mid-Cap Stocks 75
Opportunities In Small-Cap Stocks 79
Special Situations 83
Evidence For An Impending Longer-Term Rise In Price 84
Portfolio Management 87
Watch List 94
Due Diligence 95

Chapter Four: Mutual Funds

Comparing Fund Types 99
Index Funds 106
Exchange Traded Funds (ETF's) 108
Chase Hot Funds? 108

Postscript 113

Bibliography 114

Suggestions For Reading 116

Highly Useful Websites 117

Index 119

CHAPTER ONE

INVESTMENT CHOICES, CONVENTIONAL "WISDOM"

As all of us who take an interest in managing our own investments are aware, there is no lack of advice on how to be successful. If anything, the amount produced is accelerating each year. This is explained well by the good old supply-demand theory: the greater the proportion of the population that chooses to make its own investment decisions, the greater the quantity of advice that the professional investment community supplies. However, for the amateur investor just getting started, the problem of whose advice to take seriously is not as big as it looks. This is because most of the advice givers present variations on a few major themes. This should not be surprising. After all, *how many kinds of decisions must be made to succeed at investing? Only three major ones: selecting what to buy, timing the buy, and timing the sale.*
   The challenges associated with trying to make these decisions correctly haven't changed much since stock markets were created, but there has been one important change for the better for the amateur investor: information availability. As Jonathan Steinberg puts it: "Today is an extraordinary time for individual investors. Why? Because we're in the midst of a genuine investing information explosion... In an earlier era, only affluent people had enough resources and contacts to stay in the know... *Information moves markets*, and an individual investor today can be better informed about a particular company than J.P. Morgan was in his heyday" (*Midas Investing*, pp. xii, xiii).

In this book I will criticize the most frequently given pieces of advice for each of the three kinds of decision. While I will be critical of most of them, it needs to be remembered that I am concerned with them as advice pertaining to current market conditions. Changes have made some suggestions obsolete, but it is not impossible that these will be good advice again someday. Market conditions change, and the changes tend to be cyclical. Buying only stocks whose price per share is lower than the company's assets per share might have been good advice during the Great Depression, but it is an absurd strategy under current market conditions. Will it become good advice again some day? I hope not, at least while I am an investor!

Investment Instruments

The first order of business is to describe and discuss the merits of the better-known kinds of investment instruments available to the amateur investor.

Bonds

Bonds, in effect, represent loans made to governments or corporations that the institution promises to repay at maturity. Interest is commonly paid annually at a set rate. Bonds provide much greater safety of principal than stocks. This can *seem* to be a decisive reason to prefer bonds for those who must live off their capital. But investment decisions must take into account both risk and *return*, and the return on bonds has, historically, been inferior to that of stocks. The average annual return over the long term for the stock market, as measured by market indexes, is distinctly better than for bonds. This has been documented often.

Jeremy Siegel, in *Stocks For The Long Run*, provides some good data. According to his Table 1-1, from 1926 to 1997 stocks had a 10.6% annualized rate of return, whereas long-term government bonds yielded 5.2%, about half as much. Lest you have the impression that 5.4% isn't a very big difference, consider this. If you invested $10,000 for 30 years at 5.2%, you would have $45,759 at the end. Invested at 10.6%, you would have $205,425. That's a 160 grand difference!

This comparison, valid as far as it goes, is somewhat misleading. Investors should be interested in "real return", the difference between the return on your investment and the rate of inflation. Between 1926 and 1997, Siegel reports that the annualized inflation rate was 3.1% per year. What this means is that if you made an investment of $10,000 in 1926 and got an annual return of 3.1% compounded, you would have $87,370 in 1997 (assuming you're still around). But that amount would have no extra buying power over your initial investment. You didn't make any real gain where it counts - increasing your buying power.

If the investment real return rates are calculated for the 1926-1997 period, it is found that the return is 7.2% for stocks and 2.0% for bonds. Doing our 30-year compound calculation, a $10,000 investment compounded at 2.0% grows to $18,114. Compounded at 7.2% it grows to $80,509! To highlight the difference even more concretely, if you were 65 at the end of those 30 years and converted these sums to annuities, you would get about $130 per month from the bonds and about $560 per month from the stocks (based on current annuity rates). The former sum might buy your groceries. The latter could pay your rent! (Taxes are being ignored here because we are making relative judgments.)

Stocks

A stock share is a share in the ownership of a company. It entitles the holder to participate in the operation of the business at the board of directors level. This in practice amounts to having voting power proportional to the percentage of shares held, for electing board members and making policy decisions on matters such as mergers, dividend distributions, and buyouts. The owner is also entitled to receive dividends on a per share basis. Stock markets are the organizations that enable us to buy and sell shares in an auction format.

We have already heard that stocks collectively (as measured by indexes such as the TSE 300 and the S&P 500) have provided higher returns than bonds, but with higher risk due to volatility. In view of these differences, one might think that bonds are a better portfolio choice for those living off acquired capital. But a successful case can be made that a steady income with capital preservation can be had from a portfolio of stocks.

Peter Lynch, in *Beating The Street* presents a scenario using historical return and yield data assumptions in which the stock portfolio works even better than the bonds-only scenario (see his Table 3-2). The stock approach may involve occasional selling of shares to keep income steady, but over a 20 year period one has much more principal than the principal represented by the face value of a $100,000 bond. How much more? On Lynch's assumptions, $249,140 more. Obviously, this superiority of stocks as an income generating resource will exist only over a longish period. In any shorter period one might have to liquidate chunks of one's holdings because of market dips.

Here is a hypothetical example covering a shorter period. Amos and Andy each have $100,000 accumulated at the end of 1991 when they retire. Amos buys a government bond with an eight year maturity, paying a 7% annual yield. He gets $7000 at the start of 1992 and each New Year thereafter until 1 Jan 99 when he gets his $7000 and his principal back, a total of $107,000. Andy puts his $100,000 in a TSE 300 stock index mutual fund that has a 0.8% MER (Management Expense Ratio). At the end of each year he sells off enough shares to cover the MER and $7000 for himself. At the start of 1999 he sells his fund and has $126,222. This happens to equate to making a 3% annual return in addition to the annual $7000. Looking at the matter another way, Andy could have taken home $9,100 each year and still ended up with $107,000, just like Amos. This would be a 30% better return!

While it appears that the index fund approach is better financially, we must recognize that there is a psychological price that one might have to pay for the extra income. Our example illustrates it nicely: on three occasions when Andy draws out his

$9,100, some of his principal has been lost. On 1 Jan 93, for example, it is down to about $95,000. Could it be down to $90,000, or worse the following year? Sure. But this is all part of the challenge of adopting a buy-and-hold strategy. The validity of the strategy for the long term is attested by past market patterns. If we ask advocates of the strategy (we usually want to do this when the market has suffered a major downturn) how they know the market will go up over the long term, their answer is a good one: "Because it always has!" If Andy has trouble keeping the faith, he would be advised to have his broker or bank buy his fund for him and just direct them to send him a check each New Year's, and never look at the NAV of his fund or follow market action.

The Stock-Bond Portfolio

Perhaps a combination of stocks and bonds would give us the best features of both kinds of instrument, without the disadvantages? For most professionals, this blend is the de facto concept of what an investment portfolio ought to be. Investment advisors advocate that the percentage of each has to be different for different investor needs and tolerance for risk. Thus, it is said that younger people can have a higher proportion of stocks than those approaching retirement who need their holdings to supplement formal pensions. The former might hold 60% stocks, they might say, whereas the latter should have only 20% in stocks. These numbers reflect the view that stocks are intrinsically more volatile, and the assumption that investors will have a low turnover in their portfolio. This portfolio philosophy perhaps represented good advice when the only people who had significant portfolios were the well-off, who would have their brokerage firm manage their money. These days a much higher percentage of the public has portfolios, often in the form of tax-sheltered retirement accounts (IRA's in the U.S., RRSP's in Canada) at a bank. One can have a portfolio of stocks and bonds actively managed, but more often than not one's bank expects one to initiate changes in holdings.

The classical stock-bond portfolio was supposed to have two main virtues: less volatility of return and conservation of assets. By holding a high proportion of bonds, one is supposed to be protected from serious stock market corrections, because good bonds cannot lose their face value. This feature of bonds gave then more appeal back in the 1930's after the 1929 crash, but since then we have been able to reduce this kind of threat by creating government bodies such as the Securities and Exchange Commission (SEC) in the U.S., which oversee the operations of stock markets.

The lower volatility of a balanced portfolio was supposed to be the result of combining two kinds of investment instruments whose returns were believed to be negatively correlated: "Conceptually, bonds provide a means of obtaining additional diversification in otherwise all-stock portfolios. Economic events which tend to increase stock prices often depress bond prices and vice versa. By holding both stocks and bonds the investor is better able to diversify away such risks" (Radcliffe, p.399).

The data for Canada indicates that there is something to this. The correlation between the median return on bonds and that on the TSE 300 (represented by the "Green Line Canadian Index Fund") over the five years from 1995 to 1999 is -0.40. A similar situation exists in the U.S.

In terms of the Beta measure of volatility, the median Canadian bond fund was quite a bit more volatile than the TSE 300, having a relative value of -66%. That is, bond returns fluctuated 66% more than the TSE 300. The situation is similar in the U.S., as Peter Lynch notes: "These days, bond funds fluctuate just as wildly as stock funds" (*One Up On Wall Street*, p.59).

The main reason for regarding the stock-bond portfolio as obsolete is that the return of such a portfolio will be seriously inferior to the return from an equity index fund. The only advantage to this sort of portfolio is that one can alter one's proportion of bonds to fit one's needs for short-term capital preservation.

Of course, you might wonder why the pros recommend having bonds in their clients' portfolios, given the discrepancy in bond and stock returns. Two reasons have come to my attention. First, the more reputable reason: they would rather err on the side of caution and foreclose the chance of above average returns than lose their clients' capital. Secondly, the less admirable one: they learned this in college in their finance courses on portfolio management, and in any investment advisor courses they may have taken.

Why is this strategy taught? Because it used to be good investment practice when the only real choice of investment instruments was between stocks and bonds. In the last 20 years mutual funds have emerged as a third alternative. Even more recently we have seen the emergence of index mutual funds as another popular option.

The All-Fund Portfolio

If you find the natural volatility of stock prices makes stock investing too stressful, or you do not have time to do stock research, you can reduce the stress and the demands on your time by holding a portfolio of open-ended mutual funds. Most non-index funds hold at least 50 stocks in their portfolio, which makes their Net Asset Value (NAV) *relatively* less volatile than stocks.

These days there are a surprising variety of funds available. There are the traditional stock funds, bond funds, balanced (mixed) funds, index funds. Each of these will be discussed in Chapter Four. The most recent product innovation has been the creation of Exchange Traded Funds, such as the one listed on the NASDAQ as "QQQ", which tracks the NASDAQ Composite Index, and "XIU" on the TSE, which tracks the S&P/TSE60. These differ from traditional funds in that you buy them like stocks. They have two advantages over traditional funds: their management expense ratio is much lower, and we can buy or sell them on the day we decide to. With the traditional ones the buy or sell price is the price at the close of business on the day, not at the moment at which we place our order. This can save us money if we want to sell during a sudden drop, or if we want to buy during a sudden market spike upward. I recommend that all funds, not just ETF's, be treated like stocks, for buying and selling purposes.

Summary

As you can see, there is a wide variety of investment vehicles available to us, with varying amounts of volatility and historical performance. In general, if you want a higher annual return you will have to buy instruments with greater volatility, which means you must be more vigilant in monitoring their behavior. You may need to check on a bond fund only every six months, but with a stock like Nortel ("NT" on the TSE and the NYSE) you need to watch constantly for bad news that might bring the stock down 10% or 20% in a single day.

Guerrilla Investing?

This book might have been entitled "Guerrilla Investing". The word 'guerrilla' has certain associations that are true of the investing approaches described here. The "inspiration" for considering this as a possible title comes from the writings of Gerald Loeb, one of the most successful stock investors in history. Loeb titled one of his books *The Battle For Investment Survival*. Some would think this overly melodramatic as investment book titles go, but it accurately reflects a defensive-mindedness that Loeb thought appropriate for the amateur investor. This defensive posture took the form of restricting one's losses. Loeb was no buy-and-hold proponent. If he bought a stock and it dropped, he got rid of it quickly, even if the company had apparently great prospects. Where's the "battle" in this strategy, you might ask? Loeb would no doubt respond something like this: the battle is not in the strategy, it's in the execution! It is a battle fought on a psychological battlefield. The combatants are you as investor and you as human being. Anyone who has ever bought a stock that "went the wrong way" after you bought it has had the opportunity to fight this battle. You, the investor, may have chosen not to engage the "enemy", deciding to keep the stock because you have faith that, in the long run, it will (must?) go back up. Loeb, at least in later life, always chose engagement, and was able to defeat his human tendencies by selling.

My own experience in the market suggests to me that overcoming financially unhealthy instincts and attitudes requires personal experience. You have to go through the experience of seeing some of your stocks disappoint your strong positive expectations before you can make a genuine commitment to Loeb's philosophy of selling.

There is another fact about the strategies to be advocated here that would make "Guerrilla Investing" a suitable title. You may or may not be aware that the pioneers in the development of guerrilla warfare strategies were soldiers who faced much more powerful enemies, and had to make the most efficient use of their own limited resources. Some of these pioneers had to go to great lengths to persuade their leaders to allow them to deploy their troops in this fashion. Their superiors were often conventional military strategists who could appreciate only one approach to warfare, the one that their opponents used too. And so it is (analogously) in the "war" for investment returns. The strategies advocated here are not supported (at least publicly) by the establishment in this war, the financial analysts, fund managers, pension fund managers, investment advisors, and others who "run money" for a living. Their professed stock investing strategy is buy-and-hold, despite the drawbacks this involves. (These will be illustrated in bloodcurdling detail later.) Their portfolio diversification strategy is to have a significant proportion of one's holdings in bonds, despite the historical evidence of the relative inferiority of bond returns. Their mutual fund strategy is also buy-and-hold, while regarding past performance of funds as more or less irrelevant in the selection process.

Another aspect of the approach advocated here is also characteristic of guerrilla warfare - get in and get out in a timely fashion. When the time looks right to buy a stock, buy it. When things start to go sour, sell! Do not stay in the field of combat (in this case, the market) so long that you lose your gains or sustain a major loss. There are a number of old sayings that have been coined by market veterans based, usually, on hard experience. One of the wisest is: don't fight the tape! Your stock shouldn't be dropping, but it is. Sell! As the great guerrilla warfare practitioners knew, you can come back another day when the odds are more in your favor.

The TrendPoint! Strategy In Outline

What investment instruments should you buy? Those that offer the best return. Which ones should you avoid? Those that offer inferior returns. In the former category are equities (common stocks, in particular). In the latter category are what are called "fixed return" instruments such as bonds and treasury bills. These answers would be called "too simple" by the pros. In the first place, they would say, risk needs to be considered, since the two parameters, return and risk are positively correlated. Secondly, an investor more concerned with capital preservation needs to minimize risk, and consequently has to settle for lower returns.

Regarding the last point, it has validity only for those who want to buy and forget. This book is not written for such people, it is written for those willing to have a continual engagement with their investments. Regarding the first objection, I think it has validity based only on the assumption that one will hold one's investments for a long time. As I will argue, and try to demonstrate later, once one adopts a good selling strategy, the positive correlation between risk and return becomes much less tight.

The approach to stock and stock fund investing advocated in this book covers all three of the tasks we are faced with: (a) selection of potential buys, (b) timing of buys, and (c) timing of sells. The criteria for stock selection are quite orthodox. We identify a stock as a potential buy if its business fundamentals are favorable enough. A crucial consideration is a relatively high revenue growth rate.

The strategy for timing one's buying and selling is decidedly not orthodox. It uses what I call the "TrendPoint!" strategy. It works like this. For each stock that we decide to buy, we buy only if it is in the "buy zone" above the last turning point, if it was a low turning point. If the last turning point was a peak, we buy after the next valley, when the price has risen BP% from the turning point. We sell a holding when it declines a certain percentage (SP%) from the highest peak it has reached since we bought it. The values of BP% and SP% are established by examining the stock price movements over the last twelve months or more. Typically, a more volatile stock might be given an SP% of 20%, a less volatile one a value of 10%. My own approach is to give BP% and SP% the same value, but one can do otherwise.

I developed this buy-sell strategy from tinkering with moving average criteria as strategies, and back-testing a lot of stocks showed that it may be the best approach in terms of a simplicity/return tradeoff. Subsequently, I was gratified to find that a version has been tested rigorously by Colby & Myers in their *The Encyclopedia of Technical Market Indicators*. (More details will be given in the next chapter.)

Effectively, the timing strategy that the TrendPoint! approach represents is a momentum strategy. However, the overall approach is not a pure momentum approach because the stocks considered for purchase are selected using fundamental criteria. A pure momentum approach involves buying stocks simply because they are going up. Fundamentals do not enter into the decision. As I understand it, many day traders are pure momentum players. The rationale I advocate requires factoring in fundamentals because stock prices correlate positively with earnings trends over the longer term, and a company whose stock has upward momentum without a longer-term positive earnings trend is bound to lose price momentum before long. Such stocks have usually derived their momentum from a single event or news item. Sometimes, of course, it is an event that represents a milestone, signaling that the company is finally "on its way". For example, several years ago a press release from ATI Technology ("ATYT" on the NASDAQ,

"ATY" on the TSE) announced that the company had contracted to provide graphics chips for Sony TV set-top boxes. Because of the volume of product this contract involved, it was seen as a milestone by the market, and gave the stock an upward surge.

The "Old Time Religion": Buy And Hold

If you (or your financial advisor for you) had acquired, say, 100 shares of Nortel in the autumn of 1999, you could have bought it at about $30 a share (on the TSE). Apparently quite a few investors did, either as part of a mutual fund or separately. Those 100 shares had a value of $12,300 by late July of 2000. But that was the top. Bad things happened in the fall. In late October the company announced disappointing quarterly results, and the stock price fell from $105 to $65 in a few *days*. Was this a good time to sell? The chances are your advisor would have said, or did say, "hang in there, you should invest for the long term". If you still had your shares (being a long-term investor) in early 2002 you were no doubt painfully aware that Nortel was trading at under $10 then. Your (or your advisor's) buy-and-hold strategy would have resulted in a loss of about 70% of your investment.

The pros may object that I am selecting a special case to show them up, but a similar scenario was played out for most high tech stocks in 2000. The phenomenon came to be called the "tech bubble". Similar bubbles have occurred in other sectors in the past. Many of the older advisors and analysts did not succumb to internet mania because they used traditional valuation principles, and if you had such a person you probably feel grateful for their guidance. But make no mistake about it, you would have missed a special opportunity to enrich your portfolio. The main theme of this book is to show how that could have been done. But before describing how it would work in this particular case, let's examine the case made by the investment establishment for the buy-and-hold approach.

On any given day, the popular press provides us with at least one investment advice piece from an investment professional extolling the virtues of a buy-and-hold approach to stock investing. The frequency of such pieces seems to increase when the markets are down or going down, for obvious reasons. Fund managers and fund salespersons have a vested interest in having us stick with our fund holdings come hell or high water. There is not just their immediate loss of management fees and commissions, of course. There is their interest, which their clients share, in having an orderly market. A stampede of fund redeemers requires fund managers to sell stocks on a massive scale into a falling market. Given the size of their holdings it is impossible for managers to unload quickly without driving prices down farther. A panic among fund holders can destroy an awful lot of market capitalization. Though stock market meltdowns do not generally damage the economy in the short run, people who are locked into the markets through their pension plans can sustain serious and permanent damage to their future standard of living.

It is said that stock markets are driven by two emotions, fear and greed. The above considerations clearly represent an appeal to fear and are, to my mind, the strongest reasons for adopting the buy-and-hold strategy. The last one even has moral force. However, the advice givers commonly give reasons that appeal more to greed. Perhaps they think this is a more persuasive approach, because it appeals to self-interest.

The classical advice on buying and selling can be expressed as: "Buy stocks of good companies at reasonable prices and hold them for the long term." Unpacking this a bit, a "good company" is one with good fundamentals, a "reasonable price" is a price such that the price/earnings ratio (P/E) is not too high. By "long term" is meant at least three years. What does this advice have going for itself?

First of all, the formula seems to be suspiciously like the advice Will Rodgers gave: "Don't speculate. Buy a good stock and hang onto it, and if it don't go up don't buy it." Rodgers' point is, of course, about the difficulty of identifying stocks that will go up long-term. At the time of writing, the TSE 300 had risen 120% over the last five years. Only 133 companies on the TSE have done better, out of a 1000 or so currently listed.

Given that selecting stocks that will rise steadily over the long term is more difficult than selecting them for a shorter term, we might ask what reasons can be given in support of this strategy. One of the reasons often given is that, according to the experts, studies show that buy-and-hold pays off in the long run. However, we might wish to know how long that "long run" will be and how big the payoff is. The famous economist and successful stock investor John Maynard Keynes noted that "in the long run we are all dead"! For most people a long run of 30 years is near the maximum, since most do not start investing until they are in their 30's. What annual return should we expect from a buy-and-hold approach for an appropriately diversified portfolio of stocks over 30 years? Well, the Standard & Poor's 500 Index closed out 1968 at about 100. At the end of 1998, 30 years later, it was at 1229. That is an annualized rate of return of 8.72%. The Dow-Jones Industrial Average has returned a bit less, as has the TSE 300. One might, then, hope to manage about 8% or so per year by buying a selection of blue-chip stocks and hanging on to them for years.

Obviously, since they recommend the buy-and-hold strategy, the money managers think that this is a satisfactory return, although chances are you think it a bit low. But it is indeed high relative to returns from other investment vehicles such as bonds and treasury bills as we saw. With them you can expect "in the long run" about 4% to 5%.

Can The Markets Be Timed?

A second reason given for not trading, but holding for the long term, is that no one can successfully time the market consistently. The pros may be able to spot a significant upturn or downturn sometimes, but not consistently. Elaine Garzarelli, an investment firm vice-president in New York, became famous, at least briefly, by forecasting the October 1987 crash on the NYSE. As Malkiel tells it "Turning bearish in August, she was recommending by September 1 that her clients get completely out of the stock market. By October 11 she was almost certain that a crash was imminent. Two days later ... she told *U.S.A Today* that a drop of more than 500 points in the Dow-Jones averages was coming. Within a week, her predictions were realized." (*A Random Walk Down Wall Street*, p.150) We don't hear how many of her clients took her advice, but her suddenly-acquired extra credibility was lost to some degree when, after the crash she predicted that there would be another loss of 200 to 400 points. It didn't happen and the market bounced back, and the funds she managed underperformed badly in 1988.

So is it impossible to consistently succeed at timing markets? I want to argue that TrendPoint! does enable us to do so, by presenting an illustration of how it is done.

Those of us interested in higher-growth stocks find that most are listed on the NASDAQ, so we pay more attention to the NASDAQ 100 Index. There is a tracking stock for this index, trading on the NASDAQ as "QQQ". In a real sense, therefore we can "buy the market", so that a strategy that provided buy and sell points that resulted in superior returns to the buy-and-hold approach would prove that markets can be timed.

Suppose, then, that we bought 100 shares of QQQ on 02 Jan 01 (to pick a random, but convenient, date). To use TrendPoint! we need to settle on a SP% and BP%. On trying several BP/SP% figures for QQQ during 2000, I found that a value of 10% would give the best return over the year. Using this figure, I could buy 100 shares at the opening on 02 Jan 01 for $58.56 each, $5856 plus $25 commission for a total outlay of $5881. During the year this money would be totally invested after each sale arising from the price dropping 10% intra day from the last peak closing value. At the close of business on 31 Dec 01 I would hold 157 shares valued at $38.91 each, a total of $6109. Along the way I would have made 12 additional trades, which would have cost a total of $300 commission, so I would actually have $5809 in assets invested. This represents a return of minus 1.22%.

This return easily beats the return of the NASDAQ market, as the index lost 33.6% over the year. This is the return a buy-and-hold strategy would have provided.

This is not a specially selected case. In general, TrendPoint! will give a better return than buy-and-hold whenever a stock has a lower value at the end of the year than at the start. The only time buy-and-hold will match TrendPoint! is when a stock rises steadily. In such a case, TrendPoint! will have us buying and holding because the price does not fall to a sell point. This seldom happens over longer periods. No matter how well a company is progressing, there will be unrelated factors such as market sentiment that will cause the price to fall at some time or other.

The Trading Ineptness of the Amateur

Another reason commonly given to persuade you not to sell off when your stocks begin to "tank" is that amateur investors, it is alleged, are inclined to be governed more by fear and greed than the pros, which is supposed to lead to selling off when the market is at the bottom (fear driven) and buying at the top (greed inspired). The only data I have seen to support this unflattering hypothesis are the odd-lot trading patterns.

Stocks normally trade in minimum blocks of 100 shares, regardless of share price. The people who buy in quantities of less than 100 shares are the small investors, who might want some Microsoft but can't afford 100 shares. Hence, they buy an odd lot. The collective behavior of odd-lot buyers has been so consistent in mistiming stock trades that savvy traders use this behavior as a guide to when to do the *opposite*. As William O'Neil notes, "If you will compare the bottoms of all prior bear markets, you will see that in almost every case there was a substantial increase in emotional odd-lot short selling" (*How To Make Money In Stocks*, 2nd ed., p. 72).

Now it may well be the case that most small investors do time the market poorly, but this may be due in part to their not having a system for buying and selling. On the other hand, some may indeed have a system, but succumb to the temptation to set it aside when under strong psychological pressure. Providing the latter group with one more trading system won't help them, they need to make psychological adjustments, or put their stock transactions in the hands of a competent professional who will resist their untimely urges.

Prohibitive Trading Costs?

The last argument put forward for the buy-and-hold strategy is that, even if one could sell near the top and buy near the bottom, the price swings would require frequent trading, which would incur brokerage fees that would eat up one's profits. But this need not be the case anymore. Financial advisors still talk as if this were so, but it isn't: "Jumping in and out of stocks costs too much in fees, spreads, and taxes to be profitable, even assuming you could time your trades successfully" (Graja & Ungar, p. 220).

One of the best introductions to how stock markets work was written by Louis Engel and first published in 1953 as *How To Buy Stocks*. It is deservedly popular, so popular that I suspect that Mr. Engel made more money from his book than in the market! At any rate, in the latest edition, which came out in 1983, the chapter entitled "What It Costs To Buy Stocks" contains these words: "If your transaction is a modest one - say, an investment of $2000 or $3000 - the commission is apt to be somewhere near 3% from a full service broker." (p.58) If, say, you made even six trades in and out of a stock in a year, beginning with $2500, commissions would consume at least $450 (2500 x 0.03 x 6). So you would need an 18% return to just break even. Sounds counterproductive, and it is. However, the deregulation of commissions in the U.S. and Canada starting in 1975 (in the U.S.) has undermined the force of this argument significantly. And the advent of World Wide Web trading has further improved the trader's chances of making money in stocks. These days, in the U.S., one can buy or sell a stock on the web for a flat fee of $10 or less! Currently, here in Canada I can buy and sell $2500 worth of stock for $25. If I were in and out of that stock six times in a year, my commissions would be $150. This cost can be offset by a 6.72% return. So the precipitous fall in trading costs makes a stock timing approach feasible at last. (It has always been feasible for the pros. When buying and selling huge blocks of stock, one can negotiate a much lower fee. As Engel noted a long time ago: "if you're really a big operator, with a transaction involving $100,000 or more, you might well bargain yourself into a commission that is only a fraction of 1%" (p. 59).) And because of the stimulation from RRSP and IRA investing, the fee situation is even better for mutual funds than for stocks. The bank I have my self-directed RRSP with lets me trade their own funds for free, when I transact on their website, and gives me the opportunity to buy many other funds for a flat $40 fee, payable only on selling. So finally we have (nearly) a level playing field for pros and amateurs, and the stage is set for the small investor to reject the old buy-and-hold strategy.

The Nortel Example Again

Earlier I described what happened to those who followed the buy-and-hold advice after buying Nortel in late 1999 for around $30 on the TSE. By holding through thick and thin, they would have lost 70% of their investment by the spring of 2002. I also said that the Nortel price bubble, driven by massive demand for shares, represented a rare opportunity for capital gain. One way to realize the gain is to use the TrendPoint! approach. It would work like this.

The first consideration for a TrendPoint! user who is interested in buying a particular stock is to identify the optimum BP/SP%. Relying on stock price movements prior to the fall of 1999 would lead me to choose a value of 25%. This is higher than what would be found appropriate for many stocks, but Nortel is, and was, relatively volatile.

Suppose, for example that we TrendPoint! users bought 100 shares at $30 on 02 Sep 99. The stock price ramped up to a peak of $104.175 (closing price) on 27 Mar 00, but began dropping after that. Our SP would be 0.75 x 104.175 or 78.13. The stock's closing price first fell below this when it closed at 76.00 on 12 Apr 00. TrendPoint! dictates that we sell the following day, regardless of opening price. It opened at 78.00 on 13 Apr 00, and we suppose we sell at that price. Our initial $3000 has become $7800, not just on paper, but in our account. The drop seemed due to an overall NASDAQ drop, not to anything specific about Nortel, so we monitor its price. On Apr 14 00 it closes at 68.225. From there its BP would be 1.25 x 68.225, or 85.28. At that price, TrendPoint! says, a new upward trend would have been established. On 13 Apr 00 it closes above this value so we buy at the open the next day, which is 83.00. Supposing we invest our entire $7800, we get 94 shares. After this, the stock ratchets upward and peaks at 123.10 on 26 Jul 00. From this point our SP is 0.75 x 123.10, or 92.33. It first falls through this value on 27 Sep 00, so we sell for 88.30 on 28 Sep 00. Our proceeds would be 88.30 x 94, or $8300. Altogether, we have made four trades, which would cost about $25, for a total of $100. Subtracting that from the $8300 we have a net of $8200. *Our return since 02 Sep 99 is 8200/3000, or 173%.* This represents an annualized return of 156%. We continue to monitor Nortel watching for a trend to become established off a bottom, but things go from bad to worse and the price does not get to a BP until 22 Jan 01. Do we buy then? Remember, TrendPoint! does not compel buying, only selling. Given all the bad news since we sold in late September, I doubt that we would. It is clearly better to walk away with our $5200 profit.

You might suggest that a really good selling procedure would have us selling nearer the top, the $123.10 reached in July. Alas, I know of no satisfactory system that would dictate that. One might sell near the top on instinct, and be better off, but instincts do not yield consistency. Why doesn't TrendPoint! get us out nearer the top? Because the downward trend does not become clearly identifiable until later. Nortel is a volatile stock, and changes in share price of less than 25% do not necessarily show a trend. In adopting any selling rule we must face up to this brute fact: *tops are identifiable only after they have gone by.*

Conclusion

As I look back on my learning experience in investing I can see now that I was almost entirely concerned with learning how to pick good stocks. After managing to convert some very good gains into very modest ones, I finally realized that I had spent no time at all on developing a policy for selling my stocks. One reason for this was continually encountering the buy-and-hold advice. If we're supposed to keep our stocks after we buy them, there is no need to learn how to sell, right? Seems logical! I suspect that most amateurs who start educating themselves in investing can tell a similar story. The main item on the agenda, then, is to set out and defend a selling strategy.

CHAPTER TWO

SELLING

"Stocks are made to be sold as well as bought. Only a complete combination of these two actions, each reasonably well executed, results in a profit."-- Donald Cassidy

Most readers will find it odd to be reading about selling before being given any advice on buying. There are several reasons for this novel sequence. First, you only have a real profit after you sell. Second, the process of selecting and buying a stock is such that one loses some of one's objectivity in judging its subsequent performance. This produces a dangerous reluctance to sell when selling is the correct thing to do, which can undermine profit. This psychological problem is compounded by the prevalence of buy-and-hold advice from the pros, in books for the amateur investor, magazines, and newspapers. Personally, all of my major losses occurred before I de-programmed myself away from that old buy-and-hold religion. In short, I am covering selling before buying because *selling is more psychologically challenging and more important financially than buying.*

Not all books and articles on stock investing neglect selling strategies, but their advice is generally vague or skimpy. Nearly all of them do not stress that the main problems in successful selling are psychological. To my mind, the best book covering selling, by far, is Donald Cassidy's *It's When You Sell That Counts*. Cassidy's coverage of the psychological impediments to successful selling is unexcelled, and I will be relying on his work in what follows.

Selling By Target Price

One suggestion is that one ought to decide on a target price for selling when one buys. This seems to be a favorite of the analysts who work for the fund managers and institutional money managers. The idea is to arrive at a fully-valued price, buy when the stock is appreciably below that figure, then sell when it climbs to that value. There are several drawbacks to this approach, one being that one may sell prematurely, perhaps missing the big profits. This is most likely to happen with stocks that reach high price-earnings (P/E) ratios. An extreme example from a few years ago is Amazon, the web bookseller. An analyst who examined this company in early June 1998 when the stock was $45 decided to recommend their stock with a very aggressive target price of $90 expected to be reached by the end of the year. Subsequently, the stock shot to $90 before the end of June! The analyst was as surprised as anyone, and given that Amazon had not made a profit yet, they recommended selling. After all, we shouldn't get too greedy. Well, those who followed the analyst's recommendations made a nice profit, but then again, five months later Amazon closed at $153.25! The lesson is clear: don't lock yourself into a fixed selling price, *let the winners ride*. Pros who set sell targets are almost always relying exclusively on company fundamentals, but market demand isn't wholly determined by fundamentals, especially now that momentum trading has become somewhat respectable. So stock prices can go way beyond what fundamentals imply. To take advantage in such cases we need to rely on price movements to determine selling points. TrendPoint! allows us to do this.

This last piece of advice conflicts with an alternative policy advocated by several writers, including Cassidy, which can be expressed like this: if you wouldn't buy the stock at this price, then you should sell it. Implementing this strategy requires us to select a highest-price that we would be willing to pay, then selling when the stock reaches it. But the strategy relies on a dubious assumption, that *we* are in a position to know what the stock is worth. This assumption contrasts with another: a stock is worth what people are willing to pay for it. When we adopt the "let it ride" approach, we are, in effect, backing the second claim and rejecting the first. And if we are amateur investors we should take to heart that, even with all the information available to us, the judgment of the market should be preferred over our own.

A Stop-Loss Strategy

Another sell policy is to set a price below your purchase price to limit losses. William O'Neil advocates a price 7% or 8% below purchase price as the absolute lower limit (*How To Make Money In Stocks* p.91). This strategy is in the spirit of Warren Buffett, who thinks the key to success is "Don't lose". Given Buffett's success, it's hard to disagree, other than to add that some profits, as well as minimal losses, are needed to make any headway. Zero gains and zero losses don't get us anywhere, so we still need a sell strategy when we have a profit running. In any case, TrendPoint! provides for the protection against loss because our SP value is initially determined by reference to purchase price.

"Playing With House Money"

There are other sell strategies used less commonly than these three. One can sell part of one's holding as the stock rises, to take out one's initial investment. That way, one avoids a loss and may make some money. This is the old "play with the house's money" strategy used by lucky gamblers.

Jonathan Steinberg says this is what he likes to do: "If my $10,000 investment has tripled to $30,000, I might sell a third of my stake, thus converting $10,000 back into cash. This lets me recoup the value of my original investment, but the profits I've made stay invested ... This strategy has great psychological and financial value to me. It helps me hold a stock when things look dicey" (*Midas Investing* p.181; his chapter on selling is one of the most useful in the genre). No doubt, when one has taken out one's initial investment it is easier to make the correct decision about the remainder. One has, so to say, taken ego out of play since there is no prospect of loss. Again, though, knowing how to avoid a loss is not enough knowledge to maximize or even guarantee a profit.

A Selling Strategy

The buy-sell strategy I advocate is a hybrid one. We select companies as candidates based on their business fundamentals: in particular, their sales and earnings growth. Then we rely on so-called "technical" criteria to time our buy decisions. Our sell decisions will be based on a purely technical criterion. This is psychologically important. Basing sell decisions on fundamentals is risky because we are liable to embrace excuses for company difficulties when things turn sour. Using the TrendPoint! strategy circumvents this kind of rationalizing.

Technical criteria are ones developed in terms of stock price and sales volume patterns. People who study this data are called "technicians". Their approach is such that they are rivals to the fundamentalists, because they do not rely on stock valuations in buying and selling. Since most professional stock pickers are fundamentalists, the chart people do not exert much influence in the business. There are good reasons for this marginalization. The academics who teach investment theory generally consider the technical approach to be an occult science at best. The cornerstone of their opposition is evidence that stock prices move randomly. The technicians, on the other hand, are ready to claim that price patterns in the recent past can be good evidence for price movement in the near future.

One of the more accessible reviews of technical strategies is presented in John J. Murphy's *The Visual Investor* (Wiley 1996). His explanations of the concepts and criteria are very good. Unfortunately, he seems to present his examples as evidence for the validity of the strategies, rather than offering us any hard-core statistical backing. As such, his charts represent anecdotal evidence at best. What we need is data on what our investment returns would be if we applied each of the strategies or concepts that he covers. With the massive historical data bases of stock action and the computer power now available to the researcher, it should be possible to get such information.

There has been at least one comprehensive project undertaken. It was done by Robert W. Colby and Thomas A. Myers, who published their results in book form as *The Encyclopedia of Technical Market Indicators* (Business One Irwin). Some of their results are very interesting indeed. For example, in their study of the "moving average convergence divergence indicator" (the MACD), they found that the basic MACD "... substantially underperformed our 40-week simple moving average crossover rule standard of comparison..." (p.281). It is noteworthy that Murphy presents that tested version of the MACD strategy in his Chapter Six as a very effective one!

Colby and Meyers test quite a variety of indicators. Some require access to quite sophisticated software and databases. These will not be as useful for the amateur investor with limited access and limited technical background. One of the better indicators tested was the Simple Moving Average Crossover (SMAC).

A simple (as contrasted with an exponential) moving average is simply the average price the security has traded for during the period of interest. To calculate the value of a one-year moving average on a given day we sum its closing price for each market day during the previous 52 weeks, then divide by the number of market days. It is called a "moving average" because it is calculated for the last 52 weeks from any given day. The next day you drop the first day and add the last.

Using the SMAC strategy is simple: you buy when the share price (or NAV for funds) rises above the moving-average line, and sell when it drops below. Colby and Myers test several moving average scenarios using the NYSE Composite Index for data, expressing the return in terms of total point gains over a 19-year period, using both buy-sell and short selling. Their results are usefully contrasted with a passive buy-and-hold approach, which gave a return of 85.01 points. A 40-week MA gave a 94.44 gain, but a 45-week one gave a 111.79 gain. Of the 24 strategies tabulated as comparable, only two gave better returns. But the values suggest that results are highly sensitive to the duration chosen for the average. To use SMAC effectively one needs to be able to impose different moving averages on a stock's price history to find the optimum one. Luckily, the software for doing this is now available on the web and on CD ROM. I have used the Java program on the Canada Stockwatch website. It is quite powerful. You can display three different selectable MA's simultaneously. Another excellent site is Big Charts (bigcharts.marketwatch.com). They provide a similar and, if anything, even more powerful Java program free. It's difficult to dispute their claim that they have the coolest charting on the web.

To apply the SMAC strategy, you display the stock's price history for the last few years, then try to find the moving average period that provides the best return. We want our sell-signal crossing to be fairly near the peaks, and the buy-signal fairly near the valleys, to get the best profit. We also do not want a moving average that dictates a lot of trading, so we do not want one that tracks the share price too closely.

I have found that this method can work pretty well if the share price has some longer-term volatility. We get to buy near the bottom and sell near the top. However, it does not work so well when the stock price is flat for a while. Whatever MA you choose, it will end up bisecting the price graph, dictating frequent ineffectual buying and selling. Every stock has associated "noise", random variations around an average, and because of how 'moving average' is defined, any MA will go through the fluctuations if the stock price is flat long enough.

To get around this problem, we can use the TrendPoint! strategy. According to Colby & Myers, "trends originating from a large counter-trend movement tend to persist. Prices moving X percent from the most favorable price in the trend indicate a reversal. For example, if we buy at 1540 and the next high reaches 1556, our most favorable price will become 1556. As new highs are made, they replace the most favorable price. A reversal is indicated when prices finally drop below X percent of the most favorable (highest) price. Reversal of a short position in a down-trending market is signaled when the price finally rises X percent above the most favorable price, which ... is the lowest price during the time duration of the short trade"(pp. 114-116).

By computer back-testing of the price movements of the NYSE Composite Index over 19 years, they found that the optimal value for X is 1.6% when the most favorable price is the weekly high. This is what they had to say: "... the results were remarkable ... 19-year total profits were outstanding ... This trend-following indicator appears to warrant further study" (p.116).

Having already developed a version of the TrendPoint! approach from working with the SMAC approach, I found this study very confirming. In my own tests I used daily closes for buy and sell decisions, rather than weekly highs or lows. This is safer if there is a market correction, since such corrections can take place in less than a week. My buy and sell transactions, however, are intraday values. That is, if the highest daily close since buying is $50.00, I would sell as soon as the price fell to X% below that, rather than when it closed at or below that value. Again, this can be safer if there is a sudden downward movement in the stock. Do I have to continuously monitor my stocks to know when I should sell one? No. One of the great advances for the amateur investor is the capability of web-based investor services like Canada Stockwatch to inform us automatically by Email that a stock has reached a sell point or buy point. All we have to do is upload that price in advance. Of course this value has to be revised upward whenever the stock hits a new closing high since we bought it, but you will find that this is a pleasant task rather than an onerous one. By checking my portfolio at the end of the day I can update my sell-point values in a timely fashion, when appropriate.

The key consideration in using the TrendPoint! strategy for timing buying and selling is the value assigned to X. Like the moving average duration, return over time is highly sensitive to the value of X. It can be different for different stocks, and is a function of price volatility and your tolerance for trading frequency. If X is given too small a value for a particular stock, you will be committed to buying and selling too often or too soon, and the trading costs cut into profits. If you set X too high, you are open to sustaining a bigger loss if the stock drops. So a tradeoff is needed.

For example, although the 1.6% figure may work for the NYSE index, using weekly highs and lows and weekly closes, it probably isn't suitable if we use daily closes. This was confirmed by examining the price movements of "HIP", the former ETF that tracked the TSE 100. Even 2% generated 24 trades in a 10 month period. Assuming that 100 shares were bought, and sold as soon as the critical price was reached, the gross return was 36.58%, without shorting. But at $28 per trade, the net return was only 19.85%. This erosion can be combated by buying a larger holding. For example, I would pay $52.25 for 1000 shares, which would only reduce my return to 32.31%. This is a very nice return, but you need to make a big financial commitment and pay close attention to your stock.

A more appropriate sell-point percentage can be arrived at by scrutinizing the price movement over a 12-month period and doing a few trial runs with different values. All you need for this is a graph of the stock closing price history and a calculator, although the Java program such as that available from Canada Stockwatch or "bigchart.com" is more convenient, since it gives high, low, and close values on the screen for any day selected on the price graph. Stockwatch provides data for U.S. stocks too.

As an example I will use the TSE 300 Index, an Index for which most Canadian mutual fund companies have a corresponding index fund. Suppose it is the start of 2000 and we intend to buy one of these index funds on the first trading day. What we need is a SP% value to know when to sell if the market turns down. To get one I would examine the previous year's movements, testing several values before choosing one as my SP% for 2000.

To make a first cut at getting a SP% value, we should identify the magnitude of the "noise" in the stock price, a band in which the price fluctuates within any longer-term trend. For the TSE 300, we can see that for much of the middle of 1999 it moved between about 6785 and 7285 (closing values). This represents a range of about 7%. If we held the Index fund we would not want to be buying and selling within this interval, there would be too many trades involved. If we use a "safety factor" of 50%, we would avoid this, so let's start with a trial SP% value of 10%. And let's make the BP% the same. Now we pretend to buy one share of the Index on the first trading day of the year, and trade it using these values. We will also pretend to be able to buy part shares, to get the most accurate rate of return.

The year would have gone as shown below. Peak and bottom values are included to explain the buy and sell ones.

5 Jan 99	Buy 1 share at 6554 Portfolio Value: 6554.
11 Jan 99	Peak at 6842.
03 Mar 99	Sell at 6154. Portfolio Value: 6154.
03 Mar 99	Bottom at 6180.
07 Apr 99	Buy 0.905 shares at 6798. (6154/6798 = 0.905)
30 Dec 99	Close year at 8406. Portfolio Value = 8406 x 0.905 = 7607.

Three trades were made during the year, which would cost me a total of $75, the net return can be calculated from the following ratio: ((7607 - 75) - 6554)/6554. The return is 14.7%. (To calculate overall and annualized return rates I use this handy site: "cgi.money.com/tools/retirnrate/returnrate.jsp".

As a "first cut", the 10% SP% isn't too bad. We were required to sell and buy back only once. But notice that the bottom close price occurred on the sell day. If we increased our SP% slightly we would not have been sold off. If we were to adopt a 12% value, we would have held our position over the entire year and matched the Buy & Hold return of +27.9%. If the market had corrected in a serious way we would have been out, while the buy & hold folks went to the bottom. Let's now try a 8% figure, just to see what happens. The record would be as shown on the next page.

05 Jan 99   Buy 1 share at 6554 Portfolio Value: 6554.
11 Jan 99   Peak at 6842.
25 Feb 99   Sell at 6295. Portfolio Value: 6295
03 Mar 99   Bottom at 6180
05 Apr 99   Buy at 6674 (0.943 shares)
30 Dec 99   Close year at 8406. Value = 8406 x 0.943 = 7927

Deducting $75 for three trades, the net return is +19.8%. The 12% SP% gives the best return, so I choose that value for my 2000 trades.

You need to remember that my example, the TSE 300, is not an actual stock, it is really an index composed of 300 stocks. As such, it exhibits less volatility than most stocks. With less volatility, our SP% can be lower. Remember, we want it as low as possible because this is what protects us if the market should undergo a serious correction, or our company falls out of favor. On the other hand, if the value is too low we will be involved in more trading, as we reach our SP and BP points more often. The trading costs reduce our returns, and frequent trading is a nuisance, even if it isn't expensive.

Now, back to the TSE 300. I buy the index at the opening price on 04 Jan 00 at 8414. The year goes like this with our 12% BP/SP%. A chart of the price history (courtesy of Canada Stockwatch) and events is shown on the next page.

04 Jan 00   Buy 1 share at 8414. Portfolio value: 8414.
24 Mar 00   Peak at 10053.
04 Apr 00   Sell at 8847.
14 Apr 00   Bottom at 8474.
01 May 00   Buy at 9491 (0.932 shares)
01 Sep 00   Peak at 11,389.
18 Oct 00   Sell at 10,022. Portfolio value = 10,022 x 0.932 = 9342.
29 Dec 00   Index closes at 8934.

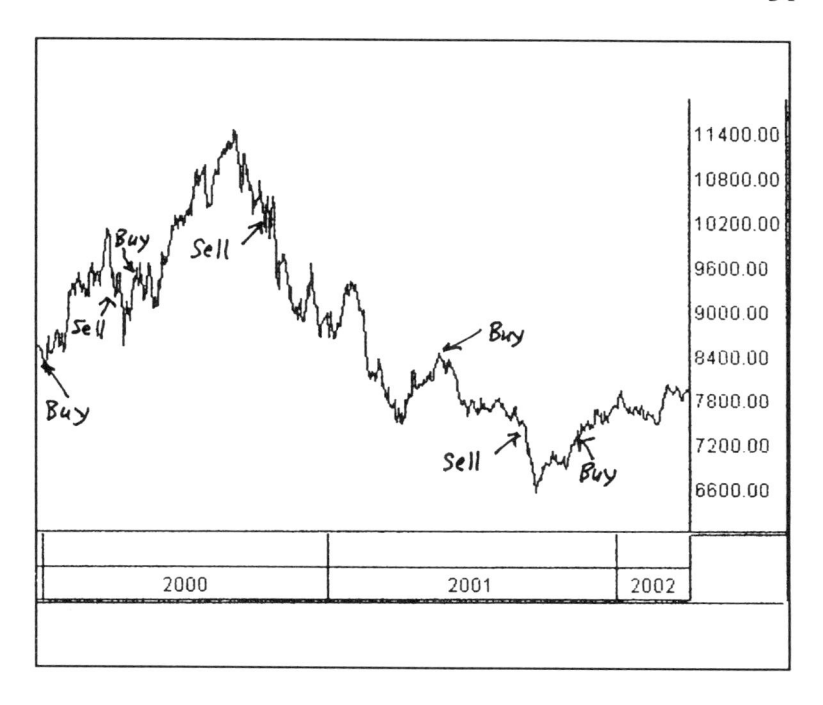

Allowing for commissions for four trades, our net return is +9.8%. The buy-and-hold return was +5.9%. Thus, we did better than the buy-and-hold people, but not just in net return. Notice that we sold off on 18 Oct 00. After that the index continued to drop another 11% by the end of the year. We would have avoided the stress associated with that drop. I cannot emphasize strongly enough the freedom from worry over serious losses that the TrendPoint! strategy affords. Even if it sometimes offers no return advantage over buy-and-hold, it always provides the reassurance that one will not suffer a major loss, if one sticks to the strategy.

As we now know, 2001 was a very interesting year in the markets, so let's carry on with our TSE 300 exercise for another year to see how TrendPoint! and buy-and-hold compare over the two-year period. Here is what happens using TrendPoint!.

02 Jan 01   Portfolio value: 9342.
04 Apr 01   Bottom at 7415
22 May 01   Buy at 8370 (1.116 shares)
22 May 01   Peak at 8395
10 Sep 01   Sell at 7349. Value = 7349 x 1.116 = 8201.
21 Sep 01   Bottom at 6513
13 Nov 01   Buy at 7295 (1.124 shares)
31 Dec 01   Close at 7688. Value = 7688 x 1.124 = 8643.

The net return for 2001 was -8.3%, with three trades made. The buy-and-hold return, on the other hand, was -13.4%. So in effect, making the three trades prevented an extra 5.1% loss. Over the two-year span TrendPoint! provided a +1.8% return but the buy-and-hold folks would have taken a 8.9% loss. Keeping in mind that there was a 42.8% drop from 01 Sep 00 to 21 Sep 01, a positive return of 1.8% looks more impressive. And again, do not underestimate the avoidance of stress provided by TrendPoint!. We would have been out of the index from 18 Oct 00 to 22 May 01, during which time the index dropped 25% (reached on 04 Apr 01) and then made a modest recovery. Experiencing a 25% drop in an investment's value is no fun, and while the buy-and-hold people were having this unpleasant experience, we would have been on the sidelines lurking, waiting for a positive trend to begin. In my experience, lurking is a lot less stressful than seeing one's investment fall 25%.

As with the moving average strategy, you can use short-selling with TrendPoint!. You short-sell when your stock falls below the sell point. When the price turns upward and goes above your BP% value you cover your short sell and buy (or "go long" as they say in the business). Doing this with "HIP" (the former TSE 100 tracking stock) for 1998 using 7% would have given a gross return of +21.76% up to selling out on 14 Dec 98, a net of about 15% if we had started with100 shares. For the same period, a buy-and-hold strategy would return -6%. This looks just as attractive as the moving average alternative, but remember that you cannot do short selling in sheltered accounts.

The selling aspect of this strategy differs from the other sell strategies I described earlier in that, as the price goes up, so does the sell point. This allows us to let our profits ride while being protected from a serious decline. It is intended to be applied mechanically. As soon as the price drops to our sell point, we sell. No questions asked! *After* we are out we can re-evaluate the stock or fund and buy back in if we judge it to still be undervalued. This contrasts with the pros' advice to the effect that, if there has been no perceived negative change in the company's fundamentals, one should hold on. The assumption being relied on here is that the stock of good companies, those with strong earnings growth, will, in the long run go up. This quote from the Gardner brothers (the "Motley Fools") is representative: "Small capitalization growth stocks ... can fluctuate by 30 to 50 percent or more in a single quarter ... You invest $20,000, it falls to $16,000 - *ouch*! You invest $10,000, now its $7,500 - *eesh*! But if you've picked high-quality, profitable companies in burgeoning industries, the volatility shouldn't faze you, as long as your company is still fundamentally sound" (*The Motley Fool Investment Guide* p. 102). But note the "if"! This sounds suspiciously like Will Rodgers' "advice" noted earlier: buy a good stock and hang on to it, and if it doesn't go up, don't buy it!

If your stock drops, can you be sure there hasn't been a material change in your company's fundamentals? If there has been a recent one, people with better contacts than you will already be selling. To cover yourself you should listen to the market and sell also. And if the drop is being caused by external factors only, such as a developing bear market, the result will be the same if you hang on. If you sell, you are protected, and if the stock does turn around and there has been no change in company fundamentals, you can buy it back.

An example: suppose you buy 100 shares of a stock for $50 each, and have decided to use a 10% sell point. For me my outlay would be $25 commission plus $5000, or $5025. Suppose the worst case scenario – your stock starts to drop the very next day, and falls to your $45 sell point a few days later. You cannot identify any internal reason why this is happening, and attribute the drop to external factors. All the same, you sell at $45. You now have $4500 minus $25 commission, or $4475. You have taken a $550 loss, which is 10.9%. If the stock keeps dropping, you have saved money. If it turns around the day after you sell, the 10% buy point rule would make it re-eligible for purchase when it closes at or above $49.50 (assuming it closed at your selling price). This might happen quickly, but it might take a while. If you can convince yourself that there are no internal reasons for the drop, you can buy back. If you buy 100 shares back at $49.50, you will have $4950 in equity, and will have paid out a total of $5525 ($4950 + $25 + $550). If the stock rises to $55.50, you would be in a position to sell and recover this $5525. If it continues to rise, vindicating your initial judgment, you will make a profit.

The point of this contrived example is that, whether the stock goes up or down after you buy it, the buy/sell strategy has cost you only a maximum of 10.9% of your initial stake. As "insurance" in the stock market goes, this is pretty cheap. Buying and holding could have cost a lot more if the stock went down and didn't come back. Even if it did later you would have no assurance that this was going to happen. This is a stressful situation. Most people cannot muster the strength of conviction that "in the long run" it will come back, sufficient to offset the stress. As one market sage said: it is better to be out of the market wanting to be in than be in and wanting to be out!

You might wonder why stock prices fluctuate so much even though the companies' prospects for growth remain steady. The fact is that while the earnings growth trend is the main long-term driving force behind stock prices, market sentiment (the fear and greed dynamic) is responsible for the short-term variations. In the greatest one-day collapse in stock prices on the NYSE, the 19 October 1987 crash, even the bluest of the blue chips lost, on average, about 23% of their market value. Before the turnaround, a great company like Walmart lost about one-third of its value. What a buying opportunity!

Market sentiment is not the only factor causing fluctuations. O'Neil notes that statistical studies show that "37% of a stock's price movement is due to subgroup influence and 12% to major group influence" (p. 219). (The building industry would be a group, building material retailers would be a sub-group.) Thus, Home Depot stock would go down, despite good earnings, when its competitors, on average, went down. This is a guilt-by-association relationship, and might seem to be a manifestation of irrationality. But in stocks it does no good to say the market is mistaken when your stock is going down. It is always best to let the market dictate your behavior, you can't have it the other way! As one well-respected pro warns us: "I can't overemphasize the importance of staying with the trend, being in gear with the tape, and not fighting the major movements. Fighting the tape is an open invitation to disaster" (M. Zweig, *Winning On Wall Street*, NY: Warner Books 1990, p. 121).

The key step in this trading strategy is establishing the appropriate SP% and BP% values. After examining many large and mid-cap stocks I have found that a value between 15% and 25% works reasonably well if one trades on intraday prices. A slightly lower value can be used if closing prices are used as trading values. Mutual Funds, as such, are intrinsically diversified, so they are much less volatile, so lower values will be found to be appropriate.

Choosing an appropriate SP% is an exercise in compromising between conflicting values. If we make the value too low, we will be whipsawed by price changes, and commission fees will eat up too much of the gains we make by selling near the top and buying near the bottom. On the other hand, if we make it too high we will be in and out of our stock less frequently, but we won't be trading near enough to the tops and bottoms to maximize our returns.

<u>Psychological Impediments To Successful Selling</u>

In this section I want to identify the most troublesome psychological weaknesses that might prevent one from selling at the previously-set SP. There are several of these, most of which are identified and discussed in Cassidy's book. To provide the proper perspective, it needs to be noted that the evidence for investors' selling behavior indicates that successful selling is the most difficult of the three decisions investors have to make. Each of the weaknesses to be discussed conspires to make us think twice (or more) about selling at the SP.

Two different situations arise. The SP is below the purchase price, or the SP is above the purchase price. In general, selling when we have a profit is not as stressful as selling when we have a loss. Cognitive psychology has found that "the pain of loss is far more significant to people than the satisfaction of gain, by a factor of 2 ½ to 1" (Hagstrom p.104).

The advice that follows assumes that you have chosen your SP% *at the time you bought the stock*. Do not allow yourself to think about increasing its value as the stock is falling toward the SP. That original value assignment is apt to be more objective than any new one you pick now that you own the stock. One virtue of TrendPoint! is that it allows us to ignore company developments once the stock is bought. You can use the time you would otherwise spend on selling deliberations to identify other potential buys. Now let's identify the most important weaknesses that can keep us from sticking with the TrendPoint! system.

When we have a profit *we are apt to experience regret about not selling earlier to secure a bigger profit*. This emotion is inevitable with the use of TrendPoint!, in the sense that we always sell below the top, so we are susceptible to experiencing regret whenever we execute the TrendPoint! strategy correctly. The danger in this case is that the regret can lead us to abandon the strategy. To combat this emotion, always remind yourself that *no one can continually identify the top of stock run-ups*. You can also try to think back to the time the stock peaked, to recall your feelings about its prospects at that time. People are not good at getting this right. Too often we "recall" that we had an urge or hunch that a top had been reached, leading us to say to ourselves "I knew I should have sold then." This is one of the most common forms of self-deception among stock investors. The fact is that we didn't *know* that, we're really just reconstructing our past mental life. Our actual thoughts were probably much more optimistic. It also helps to remember the theory behind the TrendPoint! strategy: sell when a negative *trend* becomes established, which occurs when the price has fallen SP% from the top. Until then the trend was not established, so the stock might well have turned and recovered.

A less potent factor, when selling will yield a profit, is *personal fondness for the stock*. This feeling will be stronger in proportion to the gain. There is a story told of a dying father whose son arrives at his bedside just before the old man expires. With nearly his last breath, he beckons the son to come close. The son anticipates hearing a fond goodbye, but instead the old man whispers "Don't sell the IBM." Clearly, the father loved that stock, no doubt because it was significant in enhancing his personal worth. And following his advice would have been worthwhile most of the time since the stock was first listed. But if the events just described occurred in mid-1987, the son would have been hard-pressed to keep the faith. By mid-1993 IBM had fallen to 27% of its former value. The son would have been far better off to sell when the negative trend was clear, then buy back after mid-1993 when a positive trend re-emerged. The point is: even if the stock has made you a lot of money, you should stick to your SP. Remind yourself that there is no loyalty issue in stock trading. As the pros are fond of saying in this context: "the stock doesn't know you own it". Indeed, neither does the board and neither does the CEO!

One other factor that might get in the way of selling at the SP is not really psychologically based, it is rather an appeal to rationality. It is our *reluctance to let go of a stock when the company fundamentals still seem to be good.* If you have embraced the TrendPoint! strategy for selling you can regard this reluctance as a carryover from your days as a buy-and-holder. The buy-and-hold theory tells us to retain a stock, once purchased, until the fundamentals deteriorate. This advice ignores the impact of market sentiment and industry and sector prospects on stock price. These forces can account for most of price variability over the short term.

This was brought home to most of us by the NASDAQ meltdown that began in late March of 2000. Even stocks that were not radically overvalued were dragged down with the rest.

When selling at our SP will result in a loss the psychological impediments are different. Perhaps *the strongest force encouraging us not to sell is the desire never to take a loss.* Losses can bruise the ego if we let them. This is why so many beginners hold a stock when selling would incur a loss. Apparently they rationalize holding by believing that the stock will rise above their purchase price if held long enough. This may happen if company fundamentals remain good, but it may take a very long time. And many tech stocks bought at the top of the NASDAQ bubble in March 2000, will never manage such a comeback.

On the other hand, reluctance to sell may be caused by a certain kind of confusion, identified by O'Neil in this passage: "When you say "I can't sell this stock because I don't want to take a loss", you assume that what you want has some bearing on the situation. Yet the stock doesn't know who you are, and it doesn't care what you hope or want. Furthermore, you may believe that if you sell the stock you will be taking the loss, but selling doesn't give you the loss; you already have it" (O'Neil p. 88).

If we are going to record a loss at our SP with any equanimity, we need to remind ourselves that *the goal is to increase the overall value of our portfolio. This does not require making a profit on every stock*, and this is just as well, as it is not possible to do so over the long term. It is not even necessary to make a profit on most of your buys. In *One Up On Wall Street* Peter Lynch gives an example of an 11 stock portfolio (p.16) that turns into a spectacular success if one stock that goes up 900% is added. He comments: "The more right you are about any one stock, the more wrong you can be on all the others and still triumph as an investor" (p. 16). An even more extreme case is related by a Bill Sams about his father, an amateur investor: "My father bought $700 worth of Frito in the old days. Frito got bought out by Lay's, and then Lay's got bought by Pepsi. That investment turned into more than $6 million. Every other stock he bought lost money, but that one made up for it"

(Graja and Ungar p.23). So with some luck, even one really good stock can make you a successful investor. And if you adopt the TrendPoint! strategy your losses on the losers will be minimized.

If you have trouble selling losers at your SP remember also that the loss can be made up by replacing the stock with another one that has better prospects. And if your reluctance is high because the company fundamentals are still good, you should remember that you can buy the stock back later when a positive price trend is reestablished. Indeed, your accumulated knowledge of the company can be a good reason to buy back. You won't have to do research from scratch to discover the company's strengths and weaknesses. This sentiment is echoed by Peter Lynch: "Getting involved with a manageable number of companies and confining your buying and selling to these is not a bad strategy. Once you've bought a stock, presumably you've learned something about the industry and the company's place within it, how it behaves in recessions, what factors affect earnings, etc. Inevitably, some gloomy scenario will cause a general retreat in the stock market, your old favorites will once again become bargains, and you can add to your investment" (*Beating The Street*, p.147).

One final factor that might lead you to temporarily abandon the TrendPoint! strategy is one I was unable to appreciate prior to gaining personal experience. (In this connection we should all recall Benjamin Franklin's words: "Experience is a hard school, but fools will learn in no other.") Some investors, including myself, like stock market involvement. This can make investing a pleasure rather than merely something one has to do to improve one's financial position. But there is a danger here. The onset of a bear market will likely mean that all of one's stocks drop to their SP, unless one has a *very* diversified portfolio. When the last one is sold we are out of the market! For some of us this represents a loss of meaningful activity in our lives, and if we aren't consciously aware of this prior to our prescribed SP, we may fail to carry through on selling. When I succumbed to this, my thinking was that the market "won't go much lower". At the time the NASDAQ Composite was at about 3500, having fallen from about

5500. I had sold off some of my stocks as dictated by my SP's. But a few remained, and as their prices dropped I failed to sell. After seeing their value plunge, it came to me: I wanted to be in the market, regardless of how it was doing!

Over the years I have read just about all the stock investing books written for the layperson by the pros, and some intended for the pros too. I have never encountered a discussion of this particular psychological weakness. So forewarned is forearmed. And this applies especially to those of you who are retired and are managing your own investments. Maybe you will feel a bit lost if you have to sell every stock, but remember that bear markets tend to be only about half as long as bull markets (see Siegel p.171). If you are forced to sell everything to follow TrendPoint!, put your funds in a money market fund and take a long vacation!

Now that you've read this chapter and are committed to the TrendPoint! strategy advocated here, you are equipped to meet one of the requirements for successful investment in mutual funds and stocks: *never lose big.* This is a more realistic version of Warren Buffet's advice: "Don't lose." Buffett's version is, of course, an ideal, and as such cannot be complied with over an extended period of time. Sooner or later you will buy a fund or stock that drops below your buy price. (If it's a stock and you are operating with, say, a 10% SP%, your loss can be 10%, but not more.) The adoption of this kind of selling strategy means more than just minimizing losses, however. It also means that you need not fear big losses, and will be serene (relatively) in the face of alarmist warnings from the media pundits and pros who continually warn of overvaluation, and impending market corrections. The reason these strategies can work for the amateur investor is that they are selling only relatively small quantities of shares. It cannot be used by pros who manage pension and mutual funds, because it is difficult to unload large quantities of a falling stock. It is possible for them to do so, but at a cost -- the sales drive the stock price further down. The smaller guerrilla force has superior mobility.

CHAPTER THREE

SELECTION AND PURCHASE OF STOCKS

"There are many reasons for buying stocks, but only one reason for selling – the price is dropping."

Introduction

In these times of minimal dividend payouts investors must make money by capital gains, by selling a stock at a price higher than one paid, sufficiently higher to cover the commissions involved in buying and selling. (Short selling will not be covered in any detail here.) As the authors of *Investor's Business Daily Guide To the Markets* put it: "... dividend yields on the Standard & Poor's 500 index, which is often used as a proxy for the stock market, seldom amount to more than a couple of percentage points. Most of the 12.2 percent the S&P has returned annually since 1992 comes from capital gains ..." (p. 40).

The stock markets are a kind of auction venue, so that demand for shares drives price increases, so long as demand exceeds supply. But of course it is more complicated than a simple auction for a single item such as a Rembrandt painting. In the stock market, the supply of shares is rather indefinite, in that as price rises the supply increases too, because not all shares are on the market at one time. This tends to make the rise smoother and more limited. This aspect of stock price behavior can be seen when a company announces unexpected good news. Suddenly, trading volume starts to increase and so does share price. People who have owned the shares for some time see that they can get a better price than in the past, so some sell to buyers who believe that the stock has a higher "upside" than these sellers. After a few days, volume decreases because demand lessens at the higher price. But price may still rise at a decreasing rate, since there are usually a few buyers who are late getting in. Then some people, usually short-term traders, do some profit-taking and the price falls back to some value a bit higher than before the news was announced.

Individual stock prices are mainly affected by three variables: (1) changes in the company's business fundamentals, (2) the outlook for the industry in which the company does business, and (3) overall business outlook as manifested in the movements of indexes such as the TSE 300, S&P 500 and the NASDAQ Composite. According to O'Neil: "According to computer analysis, 37% of a stock's price movement is due to subgroup influence and 12% to major group influence" (p. 218). And the authors of *Investor's Business Daily Guide To the Markets* state that "Some reckon that more than 80% of the gain or loss in a stock is explained by the action of the overall market, not by anything that has to do with the company itself. That's high, in our opinion" (pp. 57, 58).

Keeping in mind that they are talking about large-cap stocks traded on the NYSE, we might speculate that at least 50% of a stock's movement is due to factors separate from the company's financial health. This is why keeping in touch with market and industry trends is important for choosing stocks. Novice investors naturally tend to think that their stocks should continue to rise as the companies do well. This leads them to focus too narrowly on company news, and then they are surprised when the stock falls because of a change in industry or overall business outlook. This is one more benefit of TrendPoint!. We don't have to monitor company news after buying, and since selling decisions are based on share price movements only, industry and sector influences are automatically taken into account.

There are three main explanations for increases in company share price over the longer term. One is that company earnings per share (EPS) is growing. As was noted before, with a constant EPS growth rate buyers and sellers will tend to assign a relatively constant P/E to the stock. Thus, as EPS rises at a constant percentage over many quarters, stock price will rise correspondingly. (Assuming overall business and industry outlooks remain steady.) This is how investors can make money using a buy-and-hold approach. A mature company like GE can post EPS gains of 10% or so every year, so the stock price goes up over the longer term, even with variable industry and sector influence.

A second way in which share price can rise as a result of company fundamentals is if the company has accelerating EPS growth. This is a feature only smaller, less mature, companies normally have. Such stocks are much sought by growth investors, because the accelerating EPS results in an *expanding P/E.* Suppose you buy a stock of a company for, say, $100 a share, and the trailing 12-month EPS (the total earnings per share for the last four quarters) was $5.00, having increased from $4.17 in the previous 12 months, an EPS increase of 20%. The current trailing P/E would be 20. Suppose a year later the EPS had increased 25% to $6.25, and the next year 30% to $8.13. If the P/E value remained constant your stock would now sell for 20 x $8.13, or $162.50. Your gain after two years would be 62.5%, or +27.5% on an annualized basis. But it is common for P/E's to rise in step with earnings growth rates, so your stock would probably have a trailing P/E of 30 to match the last EPS percentage increase. That means the stock would be selling for 30 x $8.13, or $244. Thus your annualized return would be 56%, about twice what you might have expected if you thought the P/E would remain at 20. So the expansion of the P/E multiple caused by accelerating EPS just about doubles the return.

The third way in which a stock's price can rise is if its P/E expands *without* earnings acceleration. This would be caused by an improvement in industry or sector outlook, or simply by an overall demand for shares of good companies. Much of the rise in index values in the 1990's was due to extra money coming into the markets through equity mutual funds bought by people investing RRSP and IRA money. Of course, long bull markets can only be sustained by profit growth, and this did occur, but it would not account for the magnitude of the actual runup. This extra demand was reflected by a rise in the P/E of the S&P 500 from 17.0 at the start of 1995 to 31.2 at the start of 2000. Even so, it is entirely possible, through increased demand for shares, for many stocks to rise even without improvements in company performance. There's nothing like buying one's stocks at the onset of a bull market! In this connection the pros have a saying: "Don't confuse genius with a bull market!"

The Universe Of Stocks

The universe of choice in the U.S. and Canadian equity markets can be divided into four groups, based on market capitalization (current share price x number of shares issued): (1) micro caps, (2) small caps, (3) medium caps, and (4) large caps. There is some arbitrariness in assigning cutoff points for each group, but certain ranges can be defended as being appropriate. I will use the following definitions: micro caps: under $100 million, small caps: $100 million to $250 million, medium caps: $250 million to $1 billion, large caps: above $1 billion.

Various considerations recommend this classification scheme. Not counting the micro caps, the categories collectively include all but 15 of the TSE 300 membership, which arguably represents the stock universe for serious investors in Canadian stocks. The 130 large caps include all but three of the stocks in the TSE 100, the large cap performance benchmark for success in pension equity funds and large cap mutual funds, at least until the "S&P/TSE 60" was created.

The lower end of the small cap segment, $100 million, was chosen because all but about 15 of the companies in the TSE 300 have market caps above this. As a result, it can be said that the TSE 300 does not generally contain micro caps, which seems conceptually appropriate. The upper end value of the small cap category, $250 million, was chosen using U.S. statistics. Using Yahoo's database, it was found that of the universe of U.S. stocks with market caps below $100 million, only 25% are followed by analysts sufficiently closely to warrant their assigning buy/hold/sell ratings. By contrast, 75% of the ones with market caps between $100 million and $250 million, are rated by at least one analyst. For ones between $250 and $500 million, about 83% are covered. From this data I infer that $250 million represents a threshold above which analysts seriously follow stocks. This is by far the most interesting criterion for a threshold between small caps and larger-caps, since achieving really high rates of return can be done only when stocks are not efficiently priced. And this is true, in general, only of stocks that are not followed by many analysts.

Thus, we can consider the market cap range of $100 to $250 million as the range in which the first analysts start to pay attention to companies, and this makes a good informal definition of the small cap range if we are to argue that the best gains are to be made by buying small caps.

As regards the micro-caps, because of price volatility, unavailability of information to the public, and their sheer speculative nature, I do not consider these to be legitimate candidates for a serious portfolio. Thus, I will not discuss them further. If you really enjoy trading these, set up a separate "gambling" portfolio. Do not spend much time in picking such stocks. The time is much more usefully spent on your core portfolio.

So how many stocks are there in these various categories? As of mid-May 2002 the numbers breakdown for the major markets is as follows (I ignore the exchange rate factor, since most analysts on both sides of the border rate primarily companies listed on their domestic markets.):

MARKET	MICRO	SMALL	MEDIUM	LARGE
NYSE/AMEX	1700	400	650	1000
NASDAQ NAT'L	2400	600	680	330
TSE	1900	180	170	170
TOTALS	6000	1180	1500	1500

For our main portfolio, there is a pool of about 3000 stocks to pick from. Put this way, the selection process may seem daunting, but the various on-line screening programs makes the narrowing-down job much easier than it used to be. For example, if we want to select growth stocks, ones listed on the TSE with, say, 20% annual revenue growth over the last three years, "globeinvestor.com" screens reveal that there are only 22 of them in mid-May 2002. Comparable results are found for the U.S. markets.

Dangerous Sectors

Traditionally, companies listed on North American stock exchanges have been classified by sector and, within sectors, by industry. The need for such classifications should be obvious. The most valid comparative data for stock selection is seldom the data for the large indexes like the S&P 500 or the TSE 300. We usually need to compare a company with others in the same industry to get anything meaningful.

The Toronto Stock Exchange previously recognized 14 sectors in their indexes. Morningstar recognizes 10. The most famous stock classifier, Standard & Poor's, recognizes 10 sectors, and subdivides sectors into a total of 125 industries. *Investor's Business Daily* recognizes 19 "groups" and 197 "subgroups". The TSE has recently moved to a version of the Standard & Poor's classification. Obviously, whatever these organizations call them, they all distinguish between a genus (sector) and species (industry) within it. Using S&P's terminology, it has been found that the most important external influence on a stock is its industry, rather than its sector, as this observation by O'Neil makes clear: "Studies have shown that 37% of a stock's price movement is due to the influence of its subgroup [industry], and another 12% to its major group [sector]" (O'Neil p. 79).

In this section I want to recommend some additional screens that exclude companies in certain sectors. In particular, gold production, other mineral production, and the oil and gas industry. As of early 2000, these represented about 100 of the 550 TSE companies that have market caps above $100 million.

The reason for excluding gold shares from your portfolio is that the price of gold is determined by international events such as announcements of gold sales by national banks, and general worldwide demand for gold as a store of value and for industrial and jewelry manufacturing. Investing astutely in gold stocks requires a different approach than investing in companies engaged in manufacturing or service providing. For one thing, even small shifts in the international price can have a big impact on the financial health of gold producers. Every gold mining operation has a break-even value for the gold it produces. If the price of gold suddenly falls below that price, the company has to operate at a loss, or shut down the mine temporarily. Needless to say, profit margins can vary a lot, and this gets reflected in stock price volatility.

The main point for investors is that gold stocks do not correlate well with the overall market, being driven by different factors. You can confirm this for yourself by comparing the TSE "Gold and Precious Metals Index" with the TSE 300. Unless you want to learn how the industry works, investment in gold should be done through a mutual fund. If you do want to learn, a good place to start is *The Gold Book*, by Pierre Lassonde. As for funds, one of the best Canadian ones is "Royal Precious Metals".A comparable U.S. fund is "Vanguard Precious Metals". Be aware that gold funds have done relatively poorly over the last ten years, besides being highly volatile. If there is any virtue in investing in gold stocks, it resides in the fact that they tend to rise as the overall market becomes bearish, but if we use the selling strategy advocated in this book, there is no need to preserve capital by putting money in gold. We simply sell off when our stocks fall to a predetermined level when the overall market falls.

The factors governing the revenues of companies mining materials other than gold (copper, nickel, etc.) are quite different, in part because these minerals do not function as a store of value.

Their main uses are industrial, so revenue is a function of worldwide economic conditions. This industry is cyclical for this reason. I suggest you take to heart the advice of Peter Lynch, unless you are willing to study the sector: "It's perilous to invest in a cyclical without having a working knowledge of the industry (copper, aluminum, steel, autos, paper, whatever) and its rhythms" (*Beating The Street*, p. 234). If you want to invest buy a good resource fund, unless you are willing to read up on the industries in the sector.

As for oils, the demand varies for different reasons. Colder weather in North America leads to greater demand for product at the retail level, which increases revenues for the oil producers. But the main cause of variations in the price of oil stocks is the behavior of O.P.E.C., the oil-producing cartel. If their members agree to reduce supply, and keep their agreement, the per-barrel price of oil goes up. This can lead to increased activity by oil-finding companies and a subsequent increase in revenue for drilling companies, and other service companies. In general, cheap oil causes economic growth, because of its key role in industrial economies. So as oil prices drop, the market tends to rise. But of course oil industry stocks drop in this scenario. Because of O.P.E.C.'s role in the industry, there is considerable volatility in revenue, which is reflected in stock prices. So if you want to invest in the oil industry, you need to study it and be vigilant if you buy oil stocks. If you want to take advantage of the volatility, you should buy a good oil fund. The oldest, and one of the better ones in Canada is the "Royal Energy Fund", which has been around since 1980. "INVESCO Energy" is a comparable U.S. fund.

In summary, because of their different demand factors and consequent volatility in their stocks, I advocate excluding golds, other metals, and oil industry companies from your universe of stocks to consider buying for your core stock portfolio. If you want to invest in these industries, you will have to familiarize yourself with them, by reading about their general characteristics and following some of the main stocks for awhile. By following the stock movements of the bellwether companies and correlating stock movements with the news that cause them, you can get a feel for the companies in the industry. If you aren't prepared to do this kind of homework, you should buy sector mutual funds. But follow them closely, as even the funds are somewhat volatile. Buy no-load funds that you can treat as stocks for buying and selling purposes.

After these exclusions, you will find that your selection universe contains mostly companies in the following sectors:

(a) *capital goods* (aerospace, heavy trucks, machinery used in factories, etc.),
(b) *consumer discretionary* (goods and services bought by consumers with discretionary income),
(c) *consumer staples* (food, drink, health care, etc.),
(d) *financials* (banks and insurers),
(e)*technology* (computers, communications equipment, other electronics, software, office equipment).

There are three other sectors not listed above: services (janitorial, maintenance, etc.), transportation, and utilities. But you will seldom find companies in these sectors passing a 20% revenue screen, a defining criterion for growth stocks.

If you want to be able to comfortably buy any stocks from among those that pass a 20% revenue screen, you will need to gain some familiarity with the five sectors listed above. Until you can, you should pick from the sectors you do have some understanding of. Minimally, you need to understand how companies in the sector make money, what drives demand for their products and services, and what macroeconomic factors affect them for good or ill. For example, "consumer discretionary" stocks do well when the economy is doing well because the consumer has more money to spend for cars, books, clothing, travel, etc. If the economy goes into recession, these companies will not grow revenues as fast. The place to be then is "consumer staples". People need food, drink, and health care no matter how the economy is doing. A very useful starting point for educating yourself on how the various sectors work is *Standard & Poor's Guide To Sector Investing*, by Sam

Stovall. If it is out of print you might find it in a local library. It gives a two-page presentation on each of the 88 industries that S&P identified at the time of publication. The material under the "Outlook" heading will not be reliable if you have an older copy. It also discusses clearly how each sector performs over the economic cycle.

In the first few years of the new millennium, you will likely find that the strongest growth is in the technology sector. A screening on the U.S. Morningstar website for sound companies with a minimum estimated annual earnings growth rate of 30% turned up 85 U.S. companies, 50 of which were classified as technology companies, and 19 as health services companies. There were 10 services companies, all but three of which used high technology (e.g., communications services). These two sectors, technology and health services, represent about 90% of the solid high-growth companies.

If you aren't very knowledgeable about technology, beyond using your computer for typing, web surfing, and buying and selling stocks, you can learn quite a bit by going to investment websites that discuss technology stocks. There is "globetechnology.com" for Canadian companies and the large U.S. investor sites such as CBS Marketwatch, CNNfn, and Yahoo! give tech stocks good coverage. A very helpful site is the Motley Fool site. They not only cover the news, they also provide educational columns explaining the significance of what is happening.

If a particular sector is doing well but you are intimidated because you don't understand the industries, you can get in on some of the action by buying mutual funds. Scared of high-tech? Check out Altamira "Science and Technology Fund", or CIBC's "Global Technology Fund", or one of the others in the category. For Canadians, most of these can be held only in an RRSP as "foreign content", although there are more and more RRSP-eligible counterparts of foreign content funds being created using derivatives. For example, Altamira now has an RRSP version of their "Altamira Science And Technology Fund". Want to be involved in the financial sector growth without having to pick stocks? Altamira and C.I. and others have "Global Financial Services" funds if you want to go worldwide. If you want to be involved only in Canadian financials, there is the CIBC "Financial Companies Fund", which is, of course, RRSP eligible. U.S.-based investors can choose from a much wider variety of sector funds, including the famous "Fidelity Select" series. Versions of these are now available from Fidelity Investments Canada Ltd.

Evaluation Parameters

If we limit our serious stock buying to companies with market caps above $250 million (medium and large-caps), and eliminate the sectors discussed, we have a pool of candidates containing about 3000 companies. And if we plan on having a reasonably workable portfolio of them, it is obvious that some pretty selective criteria (called "screens") will need to be deployed. So what screens ought we use to select the companies that have the best prospects for high earnings growth?

One of the facts about the stock markets that novices have difficulty appreciating is that they tend to incorporate *future* foreseeable positive or negative developments, including earnings performance. This is what explains the drop in share prices when a company announces good earnings that meet analyst expectations. In such cases share prices ramp up weeks prior to the announcement, then fall on the news because traders anticipating the news take their profits. This is an example of the well-known market principle "Buy on rumor, sell on news." The problem for the longer-term investor is to find companies whose stock prices have not anticipated all growth for the next few years, not just the current or subsequent quarter. So what measures can we use to judge whether or not a company's stock is too highly priced?

Whatever might be said about the meaningfulness of parameters such as P/E ratios as measures of stock value, it is used by many big players in the markets as a screen for selection, so that it does influence prices no matter how valid it is. The point is: *the valuation parameters you need to pay attention to are the ones that influence share prices.*

This was presumably the point of a famous analogy put forward by John Maynard Keynes, the great British economist. He made a lot of money in the stock market, and offered an analogy by way of advice. In his day the British newspapers used to run "beauty contests" that involved showing pictures of the contestants. The reader was invited to vote for the best looking girl, and a prize was awarded for picking the one that received the most votes. To succeed at this and at stock picking, he had this advice: "It is not a case of choosing those which ... are really the prettiest, nor even those which average opinion genuinely thinks the prettiest ... we devote our intelligences to anticipating what average opinion expects the average opinion to be" (Keynes, p.155, *The General Theory of Employment*, NY, Harcourt, Brace & World, 1965 edition).

It should be obvious how this applies in stock picking. Keynes would try to buy the shares that would prove to be most popular with the stock buyers, who were mostly professionals in those days. As I said, he did well with this strategy. It works because popularity in stock picking is measured by demand, and as we know, demand drives share price. Thus, it is generally best to rely on the sales and EPS estimates of the analysts, rather than devise your own. Even if you end up being more accurate, it is their judgments that affect share price, not yours.

<u>Price/Earnings Ratio: P/E</u>

Historically, the most frequently used parameter is the current price per share to annual earnings per share ratio, commonly called the P/E ratio. There are two ways of calculating this. We can use the EPS for the last fiscal year, or the total EPS for the last four quarters (the "trailing 12 months" value).

Many research studies show that share price growth is closely correlated with earnings growth. You can confirm this for yourself by looking at the stock charts in Peter Lynch's *One Up On Wall*

Street, and *Beating The Street*. Lynch thoughtfully includes graphs for both stock price and company earnings in his charts, and the two lines are remarkably parallel in all cases. His charts are of successful companies, generally, but this is OK, because we are interested only in companies with a positive earnings trend anyway.

The rationale for using P/E seems to be derived from the dividend concept, the idea of investing a sum and receiving payments on a regular basis that represents a share of company profits. Thus, if we invert the P/E ratio we get the earnings per share price. If a company was not growing, it could pay out all its earnings to its shareholders, annually, perhaps. The inverted ratio would then represent the return rate on the investment. In the early days of capitalism public and private companies did work like this. But in the modern growing company almost all earnings are retained to finance expansion. The current dividend rate for S&P 500 companies is between 1% and 2% of their stock price, and most of the high growth businesses pay less or none. So there is an air of unreality about investor concern with earnings. To be sure, a business needs net earnings if it wants to expand, but almost none of it will fall into shareholder hands. Rising earnings ideally mean rising revenue, if wisely invested, but greater revenue is only of use to the shareholder in one way: it causes share price to rise. So shareholder returns must take the form of capital gains, selling the stock for more than one paid for it. At bottom, the shareholder makes money only by seeing a stock price rise.

Forward P/E

There is some room for improving on the traditional P/E ratio. One improvement in recent years is based on the recognition that we are more concerned with future earnings than we are with those of the past. Relying on past EPS values might mislead us about the future growth of a company's earnings. The company's high-growth phase may have come to an end, or an economy downturn may cause negative earnings growth for the foreseeable future. On the other hand, the trailing 12 months earnings may be much lower than the forward 12 months estimated, so the trailing P/E value will be higher because investors are looking ahead and paying more of a premium for future growth: "Valuing fast-growing companies on past results often incorrectly brands the market's best performers as overvalued" (*Guide To The Markets*, p.116).

A better "picture" of share value, then, is given by using EPS estimates for the current year. This P/E value is called the "forward P/E". This version is an improvement for those who want to use P/E as a value criterion, because it is more realistic, given our interest in what *will* happen to the stock price, rather than in what *has* happened. However, advocates of the use of trailing 12 months earnings will say that this figure is a known quantity, but forecast earnings are mere predictions. And not all predictions come true. The issue here is how reliably analysts can predict earnings two years out, which is what they do.

To check accuracy, I consulted *Investor's Digest,* an internationally-known Canadian investor bi-weekly, the 28 Mar 97 edition. I selected companies whose FY1 (current fiscal year) EPS's were greater than their FY0 (last year) EPS, and whose FY2 EPS's were at least 20% higher than the FY1 figure. These are the most attractive companies from an earnings growth perspective. Among the TSE 100 companies there were 26 such companies whose fiscal year was the calendar year. I looked to see how the estimated EPS for 1997 contained in that issue would match up with the actual 1997 EPS. In March, analysts could not rely on the first quarter actuals, so the estimates covered four quarters.

Accuracy was surprisingly poor. In only four cases was the error less than 10%. Seven estimates were within 20%, and nine were within 30%. It seems to me that this level of inaccuracy precludes making forecasts of how much a stock will rise in the next year by relying solely on these estimates. This conclusion is supported by data published by David Dreman in *Forbes Magazine* on two occasions. In the 09 Dec 91 issue (p. 342), he cited results of a 17-year study that showed that the average error over the term of the study was 40% for *quarterly* (not annual) estimates. He also found that accuracy was dropping as the years went by. In the 11 Oct 93 issue he revisited the topic, and, in a study he was involved in, it was found that 43% of estimates were within 10% of the actual.

The comparable figure in my short study is 15%, but this sort of relative difference might be expected, since he was using quarterly estimates and I was using yearly ones.

Dreman's conclusion is very negative: "Putting your money on these estimates means you are making a bet with the odds stacked against you." However, we should not hastily abandon the EPS criterion. It may be that market reliance on the estimates will cause superior performance providing the market takes the data seriously. And it is certainly the case that the relatively high estimates reflect relatively positive fundamentals in the companies. Following this line of thought I decided to do some studies to see if selecting stocks on the basis of relatively higher estimates would lead to good returns. The universe chosen for study consisted of those stocks in the TSE 100 that met the following criteria:

(1) FY0 > 0, (2) FY1 > FY0, (3) FY2 > 1.2FY1

For one study I chose the period from 09 Jan 98 to 25 May 98. These dates marked the start and end of an upward run for the TSE. The TSE 100 rose 25% over the period. What would have happened if we had bought equal dollar amounts of each TSE 100 stock that met the above earnings criteria, as published in the 26 Dec 97 *Investor's Digest*? We would have purchased 23 stocks on 09 Jan 98, and our return as of 25 May 98 would have been +40%. So it seems that higher earnings estimates may give an edge, at least for large cap stocks in a rising market. However, to put the performance in perspective we should "massage" the data in a number of different ways.

Of the 23 stocks, only 13 (57%) gave returns above the TSE 100 return of 25%. This isn't overly impressive, but does represent a positive edge. Another way of judging the usefulness of the criterion is to ask how successful it was in selecting the best performers. It was fairly successful, as measured by the fact that, of the stocks in the TSE 100, 12 gave returns at least twice that of the Index, i.e., greater than 50%, and our portfolio selected 6 of them. Put another way, our portfolio contained 23% of the stocks in the Index, but 50% of the top performers.

How about success avoiding losers? The Index had 10 stocks that were lower at the end of the period, and our portfolio included 2 (= 8.7%) of them. In this respect, the screens did no better than a random choice would have.

For confirmation, I did the same scenario for the period 05 Oct 98 to 08 Jan 99, another rising market over which the TSE 100 gained 29%. This time we would have bought 22 stocks, and the return would have been 51%! Furthermore, it included 17 of the 22 stocks in the Index that exceeded the Index return.

Of the 22 that doubled the Index return, the portfolio included 8 of them. That is, it contained 22% of the Index stocks, but 36% of the big winners. Of the 13 losers 2 were selected, representing 9% of the portfolio.

The second portfolio did a better job than the first. Picking 10 at random from the portfolio would have almost certainly provided a return better than the Index. So I conclude that using the earnings growth screens described definitely gives one an edge in an up-market situation. What about in a down-market?

An obvious period to study was from 25 May 98 to 05 Oct 98, a brutal bear market in which the TSE 100 lost 29%. Using the estimates contained in the 22 May 98 issue of *Investor's Digest*, we would have bought 22 stocks, and the overall return would have been -26%, still slightly superior to the market measure. This result is contrary to the market "wisdom" that has it that the stocks of high-growth companies rise faster in bull markets, but fall more in bear ones. In fact, it supports the thesis that the best bear market protection, is to hold stocks in high growth companies (if anything).

We might tentatively conclude that, in bull markets, relying on earnings estimates in the way described gives clearly superior returns, and is as good as the market in bear markets. So, contrary to Dreman, the earnings estimate data is useful as a way of narrowing one's range of choices, even if the individual numbers for each company are inaccurate. I think the reason why EPS estimates, despite their inaccuracy, are a good criterion is that they are highly accurate for identifying positive earnings *trends*. This is good enough for picking winners. A company whose predicted EPS growth is higher than the actual growth rate that comes to pass nonetheless still grows its earnings, and this gets reflected in a higher stock price, at least in a rising or flat market.

If we use forward P/E and calculate it for a company with growing earnings, we will get a slightly lower value than if we use the "trailing 12 months" earnings figure, because EPS is the denominator in the ratio. If the company is small and growing really fast, the forward P/E will be quite a bit lower than the trailing version, thus making it look more attractive as an investment. An extreme example noted on 02 Feb 01: Yahoo! indicates that the trailing-twelve-months P/E for Juniper Networks is 255, but its forward P/E is "only" 82, because the company is growing sales and earnings at more than 100% per year.

Since most analysts like to see lower P/E's, they will find such companies more attractive if they rely on forward P/E's, which will make it more likely that their firms or funds will buy. That is: a more attractive P/E value leads eventually to higher stock price because it creates more demand for stock. Since more analysts are using forward P/E all the time, us amateurs ought to imitate them.

P/E To Earnings Growth: PEG

Another valuation criterion that may be supplanting P/E in all its forms, at least for growth stocks, is the PEG ratio. This can be calculated in both forward-looking and backward-looking versions too. A forward-looking version uses the forward P/E relative to some projected annual EPS growth rate figure. The idea here is that a stock with earnings growing at twice the rate of another is a better buy than the other one even if their P/E's are the same. This would be reflected in its lower PEG value. Even under the classical conception of buying a stock for its future earnings, this makes good sense. If all the net earnings were paid to stockholders every year, one could recover the money spent to buy a share much sooner with the higher-growth stock. Sellers, knowing this, will ask and get a higher price. So stock prices tend to be positively correlated with anticipated EPS growth rate. The PEG theory of value claims that the relationship is linear. If a company has an estimated EPS growth rate of twice the index, its stock price can be twice as high as the index average, and still be of comparable value.

Personally, as a growth stock buyer, I like the PEG ratio for judging value, because it factors in growth rates, and can reveal that some stocks are unexpectedly cheap. Consider the case in which a company is profitable and there are consensus earnings estimates for its current fiscal year and the next year. I take Riverstone Networks ("RSTN" on NASDAQ) as an example. As this is being written, the stock price is $15.72. The estimated EPS for 2002 is $0.05, for 2003 it is $0.32. On Yahoo! they give a five-year EPS growth estimate of 40%, and trailing P/E of 68.3. This seems pretty high, and perhaps would prevent purchase as over-priced if we did not investigate further. But the PEG using these values is 68.3/40, or 1.71, which isn't very far from the S&P 500 value of 1.67. On this basis I regard the stock as a buy.

There is an easier and more useful way to calculate PEG. With a bit of algebra we find that this formula is equivalent:

PEG = Price per share in dollars / (Next year's estimated EPS *in cents* - current year's estimated EPS *in cents*).

Using this formula we have the PEG for RSTN as 15.72/(32 - 5), or 0.58, indicating that the share price is low given the EPS and sales growth rates. (The comparable figure for the S&P 500 is 1.20.) This is a purely forward-looking version, since it relies only on EPS estimates. What makes this formula even more useful is that we can calculate PEG's for companies that have a positive earnings *trend*, but no positive earnings. For example, at one point, the stock of Microcell Telecom (TSE symbol "MTI.B"), the Fido cellphone people, is selling at about $60. The company was expected to have a loss of $7.34 in 1999, and a loss of $6.67 in 2000. We cannot calculate a forward-looking P/E with negative earnings, but we can calculate a PEG using my alternative formula. The calculation goes like this:

PEG = 60 / ((-667) - (-734)) = 60 / 67 = 0.90

This capability of calculating a valuation parameter for high-growth companies with losses but positive trends is valuable because these companies offer opportunities for the growth stock buyer. However, as with P/E's, one needs to employ the concept on a relative basis. That is, we need to compare a stock's value to its peers, companies in the same industry, and preferably within the same country. In the case of Microcell, there are several rivals. One is Clearnet, with a share price of $60. It too had not yet made a profit, with a loss of $10.32 expected in 1999, and $9.84 in 2000. It too has a positive earnings trend. Its PEG = 60 / (-984 - (-1032)) = 1.25. Clearnet appears more expensive, because the earnings trend is not as strong.

The people who designed the data system for Yahoo! were well aware of this need to compare PEG values. If you go to their website (http://quote.yahoo.com), and go to the "Research" page for a company, you find a PEG number for it if it has positive earnings, and one for the industry too. If a company has not yet made a profit, they may give a value based on a negative P/E. *Do not use this number because the P/E value they give is just current price divided by current year loss.* This is not a genuine P/E value. You can calculate a PEG using the above formula and the earnings estimates and current price.

Price To Sales Ratio: P/S

Another valuation parameter that should be used more than it apparently is in valuing growth stocks is the price-per-share to sales-per-share ratio, generally written as "P/S". Most academic studies have investigated the connection between earnings growth and price movement, rather than revenue growth and price, but generally earnings growth is proportional to sales growth over longer periods, so there is a close correlation between sales per share and stock price/share too.

The traditional preference in growth criteria is for earnings per share (EPS) growth, rather than sales per share growth, but if we use only the former as a criterion, we would exclude from consideration the wireless stocks, for example, because those companies have not yet made a profit.

One of the great advances that have come with the internet revolution is the development of stock screening programs that are available to the amateur investor. These allow us to select stock-picking criteria and identify immediately the stocks that qualify, right on the website. In the U.S. there are some excellent website programs, such as those provided by Hoover's, Yahoo! Financial, Morningstar, S & P, and Market Guide covering U.S. stocks and some Canadian ones. But Canadian programs are currently few and limited. Fortunately, *The Globe & Mail* has recently installed one on their "globeinvestor.com" website. It doesn't provide enough parameter screens, but it does provide for screening by market cap and revenue growth. Let's see what we can find out using it in conjunction with our criteria.

Suppose it is mid-March 1999. The companies whose fiscal year is the calendar year have reported their fourth-quarter sales and earnings. The G&M program allows us to select a sales growth or earnings growth rate over the previous three fiscal years. It also allows us to screen for market cap minimums and maximums.

Suppose we select a minimum market cap of $100 million, and want only companies with at least a 20% per year sales growth rate. Since the program only allows entering three-year values, we enter "73%", 20% compounded over three years. Running the program gives us a list of 62 companies. Only 30 of them have calendar year fiscal years. Some of the 30 may not have had a market cap of at least $100 million in mid-March. On checking back I find this to be true of 11. So we now have 19 candidates. Comparing their stock prices on 12 Mar 99 with their prices on 14 Jan 00, I find that prices have increased an average of 66%, compared with an increase in the TSE 300 of 28% over the same period. Thus, we have an excellent return. (Note that this is using a buy-and-hold strategy. We could have done better if we sold the losers along the way.) Of the 19 stocks, there were 11 winners and 8 losers, but the large return comes from the winners going up much more than the losers went down.

Now let's follow the same procedure, but set the "Earnings" parameter to "73%", rather than the sales one. This time we end up with 16 eligible companies. The average return is 29%, about the same as for the TSE 300 benchmark. This time there were only 7 winners but 9 losers, and without one particular tech stock, the return would have been only 11%.

What should we infer from these (admittedly small) studies? First, such results cast doubt on the conventional assumption that future prices are best predicted by past earnings. Indeed, there is evidence that *projected* earnings are better predictors. In the sales growth version of the study, I was able to look up the earnings estimates current in March 1999 for 10 of the 19 companies. I found that 6 of the 9 stocks with positive earnings *trends* went up, but of those 6, 4 had negative earnings estimates. This suggests that positive *trends* are all that is needed for a company to be attractive to stock buyers. No real profits are necessary so long as sales are growing strongly and losses are anticipated to get smaller.

A little reflection will reveal why past sales growth might be a better stock predictor than past earnings growth. First, revenue growth ultimately leads to earnings if there is good management. Secondly, from an accountant's perspective, revenue is real, more real than earnings are. As forensic accountants well know, earnings numbers can be manipulated by adjusting values elsewhere in a financial report. Amounts assigned to "good will", or set aside for future taxes, or depreciation, can be "adjusted". Inventory accounting can be tinkered with. (A previous year's model in the car building business is still worth quite a bit, but how about last year's computer, or the previous version of a software package?) Revenue numbers, on the other hand, are less manipulable. There may be an issue about when an item sold can be counted as revenue, but companies know that they need to stick with a constant approach to allow investors to make year to year comparisons. And of course, investors need to know if part of a revenue increase is due to an acquisition during the year. Reputable companies normally distinguish such revenue from the rest in their financial reports. (Hint: if another company was purchased and financed with stock, you might want to calculate the "sales per share" value for this year and the last few, to judge the impact of the acquisition. Extra stock should be offset by extra sales.)

These considerations partly explain why earnings numbers are relatively volatile. Another part of the explanation is conceptual. By definition, earnings are what is left over from revenue after expenses. That is, the "bottom line" is what's left of the "top line" after the in-between lines have been subtracted. Thus, any small change in revenue is magnified at the net profit line. Suppose a company had revenue of $100 million one year, and had a net profit of $10 million. Suppose, for some reason, revenue dropped to $90 million the next year. If costs were the same as the previous year, earnings would drop to zero! A 10% drop in revenue caused a 100% drop in earnings.

The P/S parameter has some validity for growth stock selection, partly because it is less volatile and not subject to manipulation to the extent that the P/E is. I recommend using it, especially when evaluating companies that have yet to make a profit, but have high sales growth. The problem is in getting forward P/S values. Yahoo! gives trailing-twelve-months values only, and does not supply revenue estimates for the current fiscal year. This data can be found in analyst reports.

Momentum Measures

"Don't Chase Hot Stocks." This slogan is often heard as advice to amateurs. The word 'chase' gives this version of the advice an air of futility, what with chasing being something one does while trying to catch up. Most pros who tell us this mean something like "You can't make money buying stocks that have already gone up." Presumably we are to infer that the best ones to buy are the ones that have still to make a big move.

What is the reason given for offering this advice? Apparently, the pros think that amateurs generally "come too late to the party", leading us to buy at the top, rather than earlier like the pros supposedly do. Our tendency to do this is another reason why they tell us to buy and hold.

The admonition to not chase hot stocks seems to be a rejection of the momentum strategy for stock picking. Recently, however, the use of upward momentum as an important buy criterion has received support from a reputable researcher. In his book *What Works On Wall Street,* James O'Shaughnessy studied a variety of criteria that fund managers might use in selecting stocks. One criterion he examined was relative strength, which he defined as price appreciation over the previous calendar year. He examined what would happen if, in each of the years from 1952 to 1994, one bought the 50 stocks with the best previous year's price gain. He found that the 50 gave, on average, an 18.31% return, compared with 14.61% for the universe of all stocks. This was the best performance by any single criterion he tested. One explanation he gives for the criterion's success is this: "Price momentum conveys different information about the prospects of a stock and is a much better indicator than factors such as earnings growth rates ... price momentum is the market putting its money where its mouth is" (*What Works On Wall Street* p.195). I daresay that his findings, based on such extensive research, have caused some rethinking.

There are several ways of identifying price momentum. One is simply noticing which stocks have gone up in price significantly during some recent period of time. The screening software for doing this is now available for free. (See later section on screening for momentum.)

A different, but similar concept of relative strength is promoted by William O'Neil. It is calculated by taking the percent change in stock price for the last six months and dividing that by the percentage change in a well-known market index. This gives an indication of stock movement relative to the market, which can be helpful in certain circumstances. For example, suppose we notice that a stock of interest has risen 15% in the last six months. We might be impressed by this value, but if the market itself has risen 20% during that time, this tells us that there are other stocks out there that have better momentum.

O'Neil regards relative strength as very important in stock selection, so he provides values for each stock in *Investor's Business Daily*. Personally, I prefer to have values calculated for a shorter interval, especially in more volatile markets which we are now experiencing. A stock may easily complete its runup in a few months these days, so using a one or two month interval is better.

Later I will describe how we can use TrendPoint! for timing buys. It is a momentum approach that is time-independent, and may for that reason be superior to the Relative Strength parameter.

VALUING STOCKS

Now that we have identified some valuation parameters, it is time to discuss how they might be used to decide whether or not the stock of a company with rapidly growing sales and a good earnings trend is overpriced or fully priced at this time. I will cover each of the valuation parameters in the order discussed above.

Price/Earnings Ratio (P/E)

Among professional investors, there is a long-term polarization based on valuation attitudes. Some say they are value oriented, many more claim that they are growth oriented. The former are interested in parameters such as asset value, which might be said to be a company's intrinsic worth. This includes land and physical plant in the case of manufacturing operations. These folks do not want to pay more for a share than the value of the assets behind the share.

As the developed countries have shifted away from an industrial economy, the value approach has become inappropriate for valuing more and more companies. And even where it is applicable, the value criteria are so stringent as to bar one from buying shares in the most successful companies (the ones that are growing faster). An obvious case is software companies, which can have high revenue and almost no assets. In this business, the assets walk out the door at night!

The growth-oriented people, on the other hand, hope to make their money by seeing their stocks rise in price. They would deny, though, that value considerations are irrelevant to their approach. But value for them is getting the highest return for the smallest investment. And since share price growth is more or less proportional to sales and/or earnings growth, it can be said that they want the most growth for the least money.

The most famous value criterion used by people buying growth stocks is the share price to earnings per share ratio, commonly called the P/E ratio. The idea is to buy stocks with lower P/E's, because one gets more earnings for the price of a share. The pros frequently advocate buying stocks that are not high priced in terms of their P/E's (price per share to earnings per share ratio). Advisors frequently respond to interviewer requests to identify some stocks that are bargains. In P/E terms, what counts as a bargain? There are two kinds of answers: a universalist one specifying a P/E below which any stock is a bargain, and a relative one that specifies a value for a sector.

The universalists normally are not absolutists, advocating a fixed upper limit value regardless of market conditions. The closest thing to an absolutist would be someone who claims that a stock is a bargain if its P/E is less than the historical average value for the

S&P 500. Since 1950 the average has been about 14. For such people the stock of a company with good fundamentals might be a bargain if its P/E is under 14.

A less conservative universalist will make their upper limit value relative to current market conditions, such as using the current P/E of the S&P 500. At the time of writing, the value is 25, which is quite high relative to the historical average. Someone who regards this as the upper P/E limit for bargains will obviously have more good stocks to choose from than the person who uses 14 as an upper limit.

At this juncture, traditionalists will introduce examples like the Dutch tulip mania, or the South Seas Bubble fiasco, where the buying decisions were based on the "bigger fool" principle. That is, one can make a profit regardless of purchase price so long as some other fool is willing to buy the item at a higher price. They will also draw our attention to the fact that the P/E of the S&P 500 has expanded from 15 in 1996 to over 25 at present. But the tulip mania example is not that similar to the stock market. Those tulip bulbs, when purchased, were resold at a higher price. But the bigger fool who took them off one's hands got ... what? Exactly what the previous buyer got. This is not what happens when we sell a share of stock for more than we paid. Very often the price has risen because the share represents more equity, or assets, or earning power. The next buyer is paying more but getting more as well. Thus, trading stocks is more like buying a cabbage growing on the ground, keeping it awhile, then selling it. The buyer pays more but gets a bigger cabbage.

To be sure, stock prices do rise without any material change in the companies, simply by virtue of demand. This is indeed like the tulip bulb scenario, but again the reason that buyers will pay more than the last owner is not just that they believe someone else will pay even more. They believe that company earnings will grow and share the conviction with almost all other equities investors that share prices are positively correlated with earnings trends. I buy your shares because, regardless of whether they are cheap or not, they will increase in value if the anticipated earnings growth continues. And you probably sell because you think earnings growth is going to slow down and you think you have found a better place for your money.

Conservatives or value investors continually warn these days, with the S&P 500 P/E above 25, that buying stocks is risky. They remind us that, in 1979 it was down to 7, and could fall again. They will also tell us to shun stocks with P/E's over 100 as outrageously overpriced. Such stocks will, sooner or later, suffer a P/E contraction. This may well be true, but it subjects us to risk only if we fail to sell in a timely fashion. So long as our stock does not fall precipitously over a day or two, we can avoid a loss if we use a good selling strategy such as the TrendPoint! approach. The pros issue these warnings because they assume we are "in for the long term", and since they continually advise us to buy and hold, consistency requires these warnings about buying "overpriced" stocks.

Some of the difficulty with a universalist criterion for identifying bargain stocks can be overcome by adopting a relativist position, perhaps one which has as an upper limit the median or average for the sector. This approach could enable us to buy, for example, a software stock with a P/E of 25, since the median value for Canadian companies in this sector is currently 28. On the other hand, to qualify as a bargain in the gas and electrical utilities sector a stock would have to have a P/E under 12.3.

Clearly, the relative-to-sector criterion is more realistic than the universalist one, but the main problem for people adopting either of these definitions of a bargain stock, or any more stringent version, is the fact that they exclude from their range of choices most of the high-growth companies, whose shares are generally the ones that give the best capital returns. This problem was brought to the attention of amateur investors, and some pros, by William O'Neil in his *How To Make Money In Stocks*. O'Neil reports that he analyzed the performance background of the "greatest winning stocks in the stock market each year ... spanning more than 40 years" (p.3). He concludes that "P/E ratios have very little to do with whether a stock should be bought or not" (p.18). His reason for saying this is "if you were not willing to pay an average of 20 to 30 times earnings for growth stocks in the 40 years through 1993, you automatically eliminated most of the best investments available" (p. 19). During the period, the DJIA had a P/E of about 15, so we're talking about paying twice as much for the growth stocks. These days the DJIA has a P/E of about 30, so we can adjust O'Neil's P/E range to maybe 40 to 60. Needless to say, the value-oriented growth stock investors think that stocks with P/E's of 50 are too expensive, but there are lots of indications in the media that fund managers who take this view are being forced to buy anyway, or suffer the indignity of falling behind the funds that are less squeamish.

Data provided by Jeremy Siegel in his *Stocks For The Long Run* corroborates O'Neil's thesis that you have to pay high P/E's to get good growth stocks. Siegel examined the subsequent growth of the 50 large-cap companies whose stocks were most in demand in 1972. At the time they were called the "Nifty Fifty", and their average P/E was 41.9, compared with 18.9 for the S&P 500. Looking at them in 1996, it is found that *every one* that exceeded the return of the S&P (12.9%) over that interval had P/E's greater than the S&P 500 in 1972. The ones that did best had P/E's between 20 and 30 in 1972. Those with original P/E's over 30 underperformed (on average) the S&P 500, so there is such a thing as paying too much.

Given the research just discussed above, and the fact that there will be few future big gainers among the large-cap stocks that have below-average (relative to sector) P/E's, we might adopt this useful screen: *buy only stocks with current P/E's between about 100% and 150% of their industry P/E.*

PEG Ratio

Anyone who has been reading analyst reports over the past five years or so will probably have noticed that, in reviewing growth stocks, there is increasingly frequent use of the P/E to long-term annualized growth rate ratio. As discussed earlier, this parameter gives a fairer measure of valuation for companies experiencing high sales and earnings growth. For example, at time of writing (early 2002) the current value for the S&P 500 is 1.67. Riverstone Networks (RSTN), a high growth company, has a trailing 12 month P/E of 68.3. The S&P P/E is 21.3. Is Riverstone overvalued? Not if we think in terms of paying for growth. According to Yahoo! the estimated five-year earnings growth rate is 40%. This gives a PEG of 68.3/40, or 1.71, very close to the PEG for the S&P 500, which is 1.67. On this basis I would not consider Riverstone overvalued, although many pros would.

The use of PEG as a valuation measure has probably become more popular among amateur investors because of Peter Lynch, who declared in *One Up On Wall Street*: "The p/e ratio of any company that's fairly priced will equal its growth rate" (p.198). That is, a fairly (= fully?) priced stock will have a PEG of about 1. He goes on to specify a range: "In general, a P/E ratio that's half the growth rate is very positive, and one that's twice the growth rate is very negative" (p. 198).

But these sentences were written 10 years ago, and the mean value has probably risen, as the current value for the S&P 500, 1.67, suggests. If you used Lynch's guideline now we would consider only stocks with PEG's under 0.5. A quick survey of the NASDAQ 100 companies indicates that less than 20 companies could be considered. Accordingly, we might adapt the screen suggested for P/E's in the last section: *For larger-cap stocks, buy only those with current PEG's between about 100% and 150% of their industry PEG.* Even a conservative outfit like the National Association of Investment Clubs (NAIC) admits the positive correlation between higher P/E and growth prospects: "P/E as a percent of the growth rate gives you a feel for how much you are paying in terms of the P/E ratio for growth. The lower the number the better the value. However, be aware that superior quality stocks are characterized by high P/E ratios" (NAIC p.72).

P/S Ratio

Obviously, it is desirable that investors see some feature of a growing company as rendering its stock more valuable. Growth creates demand only if some aspect of it is seen as desirable by investors. But there are alternatives to focusing on earnings. The focus might more appropriately be revenue per share, as I argued earlier, and this criterion is becoming more important because of high tech companies that grow fast but haven't made a profit yet. And it was also noted that revenues are more stable and predictable than earnings. So another value criterion is "price per share relative to revenue per share", commonly called the "price-to-sales" ratio. This ratio will probably increase in popularity because of the work of James O'Shaugnessy who demonstrates the superiority of this ratio as a stock picking criterion when coupled with a relative strength value. (See p. 217 of his *What Works On Wall Street*)

As with choosing P/E screens, one cannot just choose a single, and relatively low, upper limit value for P/S and screen for eligible stocks. If you do this you will exclude most of the good companies in some industries, because the P/S that is typical for those industries might be much higher than in others. The results of your search will contain lots of telephone utility companies, but few software ones. In Canada, as of September 2001, the former have an average P/S of about 1.5, but the value for software companies is about 3.5. So we need a screen that provides a range, and because of various normative similarities between P/E and P/S, we might seriously consider using a comparable screen for selecting companies by P/S: *For larger-cap stocks, buy only those with current P/S's between 100% and 150% of their industry P/S.*

Momentum

It may be that, in the past, too many of us amateurs did not follow the markets closely enough, so that by the time we heard that a particular stock was moving up, it had become overbought. But with the emergence of the Internet, it is much easier for an investor to find out about stocks that are starting to move up. A relatively new data source is the information on stock price movement stored in various databases accessible online.

The Toronto *Globe & Mail*, on their investor website "globeinvestor.com", offer up-to-date data of interest covering both U.S. and TSE stocks. You can get a list of all stocks that have risen a certain percentage over a specifiable time period up to the present. By judiciously selecting values you can see which stocks have been rising lately. These may be potential buys if the reasons they are rising continues to be operative for awhile. I have found that screening for stocks that have gone up a minimum of 10% in the last seven days yields a reasonable number of leads. To do this you go to their home page, "globeinvestor.com", go to the "Filters" area, and click on "Historical Prices", then set the parameter values when the page comes up. Doing this right now for the NASDAQ (National Market), I select a period of one week, then 10% for the "Change" value, then click "Go". I get a list of 150 companies. Many are small, but the program does not permit them to be screened out by market cap. As a substitute we can screen for the ones that have prices of $5 or more. There are 80. Screening for those with prices over $10, we have 49. Only a few get replaced every day, so studying the list once a week should suffice. Of course, we can alter the values to shorten the list. If I change the "Increase Value" to 20% or greater, we get only 14 companies with prices above $5. So using this screen we have to check out only 14.

The stocks identified this way are ones that the market temporarily believes worth buying, and it is in our interest to find out why. If they meet our market cap criterion (above $250 million) and pass our industry screens, then we should check out their revenue record and general performance, earnings estimates, etc. I think this approach to finding stocks is much better than the practice of looking at ones that have just made new highs. Making a new high does indicate upward price momentum, but the criterion does not identify stocks that are coming back from a low and have not yet passed their all-time high. In a bull market, there won't be many of these, but in a recovery after a bear market (as in mid-year

2002) there might be a lot. If you relied on the "new high" criterion you would miss out on the entire market recovery. I mention this criterion because it shows up in several books.

TrendPoint! As A Buy Strategy

I observed earlier that TrendPoint! can be adapted to become a momentum-based buying criterion. Here is how it works. When a stock qualifies as a "potential buy" based on your fundamental criteria, you can examine a record of its share price movement over the last twelve months (as a minimum) to determine an "SP%" value, as explained in the previous chapter on selling. This value will probably be between about 10% and 20%, depending on stock volatility. This value can also be used as a buy point value ("BP%"). Thus, if a stock you own drops to your SP% value, you sell. Then, if there are no changes in company fundamentals, you can monitor price movement, and when the price rises the BP% amount from its lowest point since you sold, you buy the stock back. (This sort of thing happens when there are changes in demand arising from changes in market sentiment.)

The same strategy can be used for a first-time buy. You look back and identify the last turning point in share price. Was it a sell point or a buy point? If it was a buy point, the stock is a candidate for buying. If the turning point was a sell point, you should not consider it a buy candidate until it reaches a buy point, even if the fundamentals are good. Buying a dropping stock is a violation of the old rule "Don't fight the tape.". If it reaches a buy point and your research is up to date and indicates no downturn in growth prospects for the company, buy!

If you identify a stock as a potential buy when it is in between a buy point and a future sell point, buying may be indicated, but if the price has risen quite a bit above the buy point, you have to decide whether or not it will continue to rise enough to provide a good return. This involves price-relevant research, rather than research of company fundamentals research. Presumably, you have already satisfied yourself that sales and earnings growth are likely to continue at or above the rates of recent years. What you need now is information that is evidence for a stock price rise in the immediate future.

One useful sign for guessing the direction a stock will go is the movement of indexes. Given that overall market sentiment can account for up to half of a stock's movement, we might expect a particular stock to fall in value when any index in which it might be appropriately included falls, and rise if the index trends up. And if most stocks in one's portfolio are from a particular sector, one's portfolio can be expected to rise and fall in unison with the sector index, if there is one. This positive correlativity might be exploitable in the following way. If there is an appropriate index, we can do an analysis on its movements to identify an optimum BP/SP%. Using this information we might adopt the following rule: *buy chosen stocks when they rise to their BP, but if they are already significantly above it, buy only if the most appropriate index is itself in a buy zone.*

This rule is intended to eliminate buying when a stock is in its buy zone and the market is bearish. Having gone through the NASDAQ crash of 2000 as a technology investor, I came to the conclusion that no matter how good a company seemed, and how much of a bargain its shares were, overall market sentiment was going to dominate any good quarterly report news.

The above rule has more than subjective impressions and personal disappointments behind it, though. Siegel reports that research by William Gordon "... indicated that, over the period from 1897 to 1967, buying stocks when the Dow [DJIA] broke above the [200-day] moving average produced nearly seven times the return as buying when the Dow broke below the average ..." (Siegel, p.246).

Gordon's strategy is to buy one's stocks *at the time* the DJIA breaks above the 200-day moving average, rather than during the whole period that it is above it, as I am suggesting. Siegel does his own test of Gordon's principle and concludes that it has an edge over the buy-and-hold return, until trading costs are deducted. Then it only matches buy-and-hold. He concedes, however, that

"... the major gain of the timing strategy is a reduction in risk. Since you are in the market less than two-thirds of the time, the standard deviation of returns is reduced by about one-quarter. This means that on a risk-adjusted basis the return on the 200-day moving average strategy is quite impressive" (p.249).

Using the 200-day moving average for the DJIA is similar to using TrendPoint!. An optimum BP/SP% for the DJIA, using 2001 movement with peaks and bottoms based on closing values, and using intra-day values for transactions, is 6%. With this value, my rule would permit us to buy stocks already above their own BP's during the following intervals: 01 Jan to 23 Feb, 27 Mar to 03 Apr, 10 Apr to 15 Jun, and 28 Sep to end of 2001. This is about 32 weeks during which one would have the "green light" to buy.

One way of testing this "conjunctive" buy-point strategy is to compare how we would do trading a stock over a long period of time both using the BP timing only, and using it in connection with an appropriate index moving average. I examined Nortel using a 15% SP/BP%, starting with a buy at the BP on 15 Oct 98. We would buy 100 at $12.85, an investment of $1285, ignoring the commission. Using just the BP% criterion, we would have made 12 buys and 12 sells up to 26 Apr 02. (I wouldn't personally have kept buying once the bad news started to come in, but let's pretend to do it for present purposes.) On selling on 26 Apr 02 we would have $5580 less $600 for trading costs, or $4980. This is a total net return of 288%. If we used the conjunctive strategy using the NASDAQ Composite Index and its 200-day moving average, we would have been able to buy only four times. On all the other occasions of buy signals the Index was below its moving average. The end result is that, as of 26 Apr 02, we would be out of the stock and have net proceeds of $8846 less $200, or $8646. This represents a net overall return of 573%, which is an annualized value of 75%.

Favorable contrasts like this one are explained by the fact that overall market sentiment accounts for a large proportion of the movement of very actively traded stocks. When the appropriate index is trending down the stock will too, regardless of company performance. And a stock that reaches its BP after a bottom, despite a negative market trend, is unlikely to rise much thereafter. I recommend this conjunctive strategy to you. I am presently using it myself.

If this buying rule is appealing to you, you might be thinking: "Why don't we sell our stocks when their index drops below either the 200-day index moving average, or their SP?" The reason I have not tried this is because each stock has its own SP, which is commonly reached about the time the index breaks below the moving average. That is, this proposed selling rule may be redundant if we are using TrendPoint!. I do not have hard data to support this claim, just personal impressions.

Selecting Large-Cap And Mid-Cap Stocks

From an investment return perspective, these stocks ought to be regarded as *relatively* efficiently priced, in contrast with small-cap ones that may not be. The reason for the difference is that the business fundamentals of the former two types are carefully scrutinized by analysts. This tends to make talk about value inappropriate and even dangerous, as Gianturco explains: "But the idea that good value is signaled by a low P/E ratio does not work for science and technology stocks ...Computers watch every move that is made by every stock every second. They scan for value all the time ... a low P/E stock is likely to be cheap for some good reason. It is not a neglected or an (absurdly) overlooked bargain. Thanks to the computer revolution, the last undervalued and overlooked bargain probably vanished from the stock market forever, around 1985" (Gianturco pp 30-31).

Where the danger arises in looking for bargains among mid-cap and large-cap stocks is that we may buy a stock with a relatively low P/E under the delusion that we are getting a bargain, when in fact the stock is low-priced for some reason we are not aware of. It is strategically better to choose our stocks from among those with caps between 100% and 150% of the industry P/E. It must be remembered, however, that industry P/E's vary, depending on industry prospects and overall market sentiment. In the early seventies bear market, following this strategy would have found us looking for large-cap stocks with P/E's between 8 and 12, whereas at time of writing we would be looking in the 22 to 33 range.

Recalling the factors that can cause a stock's price to rise, two of them apply to larger-cap stocks: (1) the company continues to increase its EPS, which causes the stock to rise even if the P/E does not change; (2) factors not related to company fundamentals, such as the transition from a bear to a bull market, which causes an increase in P/E even without an increase in the EPS growth rate. A spectacular example of the former would be the history of Walmart's stock. EPS rose at a relatively high steady rate for many years, and the stock price roughly tracked the EPS history. Short-term examples occurred between late September 2001 and mid-December 2001. During this period most good stocks, whether listed on the NYSE or on the NASDAQ, expanded their P/E multiples as the DJIA and the NASDAQ moved up 25% and 40% respectively. Most of the P/E expansions were not explainable by sudden optimism about EPS growth, but from the conviction by the pros that stocks had been oversold, which represented buying opportunities, which generated demand. These external factors provide the volatility that enables us to make capital gains on larger-cap stocks larger than their EPS growth rates. Referring to the stocks in the NASDAQ 100, Michael Murphy reminds us that "The average annual high price of these stocks is about double the average annual low price almost every year; if you are patient and buy them when they are down, you can make as much money over time as the most aggressive momentum trader ... with a lot less risk" (Murphy p.142). The best way do this reliably is to use TrendPoint!. Monitor the stocks as they fall and buy when they come up to their BP. Then sell them when they fall to the SP.

Here is a good example of how TrendPoint! can keep one out of trouble and give a superior return relative to buy and hold. Let's suppose in early 2000 we decide to take a position in Microsoft (MSFT). To use TrendPoint! we need to get a BP/SP% by examining trading action in 1999. We arrive at a value of 15%

using the daily close and the intra-day highs and lows. The stock bottoms several times, but after the bottom on 29 Feb 00 it rises to a BP of 102.79 on 21 Mar 00. Suppose we buy 100 shares. From then until the end of 2001 our trading would have gone like this. The record of transactions on the next page shows the price history (courtesy of Canada Stockwatch) and the trading points.

21 Mar 00	Buy 100 at $102.79 Portfolio total: $10,279.
03 Apr 00	Sell 100 at $95.10 Portfolio total: $9,510.
08 Jun 00	Buy 134.59 at $70.66
25 Jul 00	Sell 134.59 at $69.70 Portfolio total: $9,381.
20 Oct 00	Buy 153.01 at $61.31 (the opening value)
01 Dec 00	Sell 153.01 at $59.93 Portfolio total: $9169.
04 Jan 01	Buy 183.53 at $49.96
22 Feb 01	Sell 183.53 at $54.83 Portfolio total: $10,063.
27 Mar 01	Buy 174.80 at $57.57
17 Aug 01	Sell 174.80 at $62.63 Portfolio total: $10,947.
04 Oct 01	Buy 191.49 at $57.17
31 Dec 01	Portfolio total = 191.49 x 66.25 = $12,686.

The total return over the period from 21 Mar 00 to 31 Dec 01 would have been +23.4%, with the net, after subtracting costs for 11 trades at $25 each, being +20.7%. The person who bought and held over that period would have sustained a *loss* of 35.5%. Furthermore, there would, for most ordinary investors, been a lot of worry and regret. Keeping the faith in Microsoft would have been a challenge many could not have met. Will the steadfast ones ever get their money back? Probably. The company is a highly sound operation with amazing profit margins, but staying with it in the way the TrendPoint! method does would have been a lot more profitable and much more relaxing.

The third cause of a stock price rise, an expanding P/E due to accelerating EPS growth does not happen much in the larger-cap universe, since most of the companies are relatively mature, and are more likely to have decelerating EPS growth.

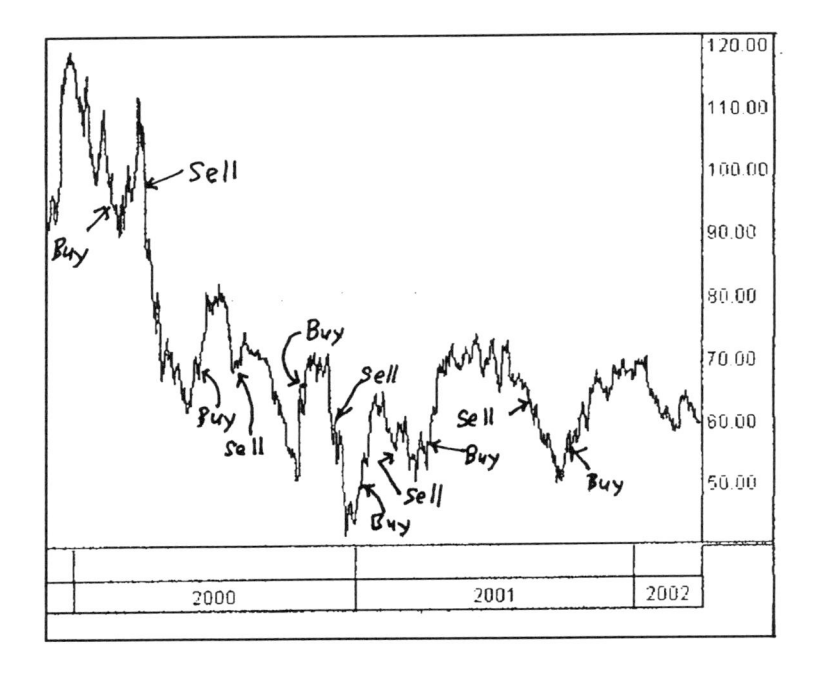

At best they have steady growth rates, somewhere between 10% and 20% in the case of technology companies such as IBM, Microsoft, and Intel.

The stocks we will want to buy when the market does not offer an opportunity for P/E expansion, then, will be ones with at least three essential characteristics:

(1) EPS growth rate above the median for the industry, as estimated by analysts covering the stock,

(2) P/E (last 12 months) between about 100% and 150% of the P/E for the industry, which shows the company's prospects are seen as good by the pros, for at least the next few years.

(3) Most analyst ratings are the equivalent of "strong buy" or "buy". This is excellent evidence for believing that the stock's price may rise within the next few quarters, since analysts downgrade the stocks they follow when they reach their target

prices. This is often reported as "downgraded on valuation", to distinguish from downgrades on deteriorating fundamentals.

(4) The stock's price is in a "buy zone", i.e. some price above the last BP but not yet down to its SP, as calculated using the BP% and SP% values you have established for the stock.

Some other desirable characteristics are: (a) A PEG close to the industry median, (b) A P/S close to the industry median.

Criteria (1) and (2) are value parameters, the third one is a combination of value and timing, and the fourth is a pure timing criterion. There may be a large number of stocks that meet both of the first two criteria, but if we are to avoid the "dead money" problem we ought to buy only ones that also meet (3). Ideally, we want to buy just when the stock rises above our calculated BP, to get the maximum out of the upward momentum that is now in place. But if it did not come to our attention until a while later it may still be a good buy.

Opportunities In Small-Cap Stocks

As noted earlier, when I refer to "small caps" I am talking about stocks with market capitalization between $100 million and $250 million in either U.S. or Canadian dollars. On the TSE in May 2002 there are about 180 of these, and about 900 in the U.S. (all markets). So there is a lot of winnowing needed to create a small portfolio. However, if we require that a company has made a profit over the last 12 months there are about 100 on the TSE and 400 in the U.S. In some ways looking for promising small-cap stocks is like looking for the needle in the proverbial haystack, but screening programs enable us to cope surprisingly well.

The case for having a small-cap portfolio has been well made by Graja and Ungar in their *Investing In Small-Cap Stocks* (2nd edition, pp. 25-27). They do not claim that we should choose small caps instead of medium and large-caps. Rather, "Small-cap stocks ... should still be just one part of a larger, diverse portfolio ..." (p. 28). My view is that they should be segregated in a portfolio separate from the one containing one's core holdings. They need to be selected and traded using somewhat different criteria from those applicable to medium and large-caps. By keeping them separate we will not be so likely to unconsciously treat them inappropriately. Some of the important differences will be pointed out in this section.

The main reason Graja and Ungar give for taking small caps seriously center on the possibilities for higher capital gains: "You have a better chance of finding real value in small stocks than in larger ones" (p.25). (By "value" they mean lower P/E's relative to expected EPS growth.) They support this claim to better value two ways. First, they present some research data.

According to them, as of the end of 1998, among all the stocks in the top quintile (top 20%) of estimated EPS growth (in a universe of 1100 stocks), the P/E for small caps was about 20, whereas the value for large-caps was about 44. In PEG terms, the large-caps in the quintile of top growers had a value of about 1.3, whereas the small caps had a value of only 0.6. Does this make the high-growth small caps bargains? Yes, if the ones you buy ultimately turn into medium or even large-caps. If this happens we can benefit both from EPS growth and P/E expansion. In the study the "Average Long-Term EPS Growth" of the top quintile was 33%. If the ones you buy do this, their price will rise at about the same rate (certain other things being constant). But if they move up to the medium or even large-cap category, you will benefit from a nice P/E expansion too, market-cap increases generate visibility and, hence, demand.

Secondly, they argue that the pros pretty much ignore small caps: "... more good values exist among these companies because so many of the big players give the sector short shrift ... Large institutional investors can't earn enough on small stocks to recover their research costs ... Brokerages also neglect small stocks ... the 2600 companies between $60 million and $600 million are each followed by about three ... The result: Many fine companies remain undetected, their share prices far below what their intrinsic value would justify. You ... gain an edge by discovering these gems before other investors can bid them up" (pp. 26, 27).

It would seem, then, that the lower P/E's of small-cap, high growth stocks is explained by a lack of demand for them, arising from a lack of interest by the big buyers. But it is not only a matter of economic efficiencies that keep big buyers away, there are also legal constraints. As Peter Lynch explains it: "the SEC says a mutual fund such as mine cannot own more than 10% of the shares in any given company, nor can we invest more than 5% of the fund's assets in any given stock ... the result is that the bigger funds are forced to limit themselves to the top 90 to 100 companies, out of the 10,000 or so that are publicly traded" (Lynch, *One Up On Wall Street* , p.48). The rules are similar in Canada, with similar consequences.

Given the reluctance and constraints placed on big buyers, then, the likelihood of finding bargains among small caps is relatively high. All we need to do is identify the ones that do subsequently meet their long-term growth expectations. To do this unavoidably involves more thorough research into their prospects and financials. We cannot piggyback on the judgments and information provided by the pros, there isn't enough of it! If you are not equipped or not inclined to get into the details in each case that passes a few basic screens, you had better avoid setting up a small-cap portfolio.

Another impediment to success in small caps is that, regardless of your willingness to do the research, the information on these companies is not so readily available. Wire services and stock news websites just do not report materially important information on stocks not widely held. You need to monitor the company website, if it has one, or phone their investor relations person. (Not all small companies have them.)

Personally, I have found the greatest difficulty is in getting a reliable estimate of the size of the market for the products of small companies. And even if there is a relatively large market identified, a larger company may start to produce the same item and sell it at a lower price, thereby driving the smaller company out of the market by being more efficient or perhaps engaging in predatory pricing. These sorts of considerations are what lead small-cap pro investors to advocate buying service companies rather than product ones because of more dependable recurring revenues. (See Broadfoot, chapter 7, on this theme.)

Another cause for concern in selecting small caps, besides the need for more expertise, is their volatility. We can protect ourselves from this to some extent by using TrendPoint!, but price changes can be sudden, in either direction. Having a stock service send an automatic warning that a stock has fallen to its SP won't save us from a big loss if we do not check our email every day. Besides doing more research, then, we must also more closely monitor price movements of small caps. The "bottom line" is that small caps are for the committed, knowledgeable, investor. But the magnitude of returns in small caps might be enough motivation to get involved.

A relatively spectacular example of what can happen if you make a good pick is the rise to prominence of C.G.I., a Montreal-based company that provides outsourcing computer services for large companies. In early January of 1997 the market cap had grown to $45million. By mid-June it had crossed the $100 million mark, becoming a small cap. Demand continued to increase, and this was explained by an announcement from Fidelity, the world's largest mutual fund company, on 27 Oct 97. It announced that it had purchased 10% of C.G.I.'s shares. At this point the market cap was about $200 million. Demand continued, and the cap had reached $700 million in January 1998. At this juncture, the TSE announced that the company would be added to the TSE 300. When this happened, there would be a new source of demand, the Canadian index funds that must hold the index stocks in their portfolios, and the large-cap managed funds. With a few slack periods, demand was sustained, and in early 2000 the company had a market cap of $8.8 *billion*, compared with $45 million in January 1997. Corrected for splits, the share price then was 50 times higher than in January 1997. If one had bought 100 shares at $12 then, that $1200 would have grown to $60,000. Since then, company value has fallen, but anyone using the TrendPoint! approach would have sold in early 2000 and retained at least 80% of their gain.

You might think that waiting for the company to qualify as a small-cap by reaching the $100 million threshold, as I might, is too conservative. Buying C.G.I. back when it was a micro cap would be even better. True, in this case, but C.G.I. was an extraordinary success story. Most other micro caps of the time are probably still that, and many have disappeared. To counter the urge to "get in on the ground floor", I recall that Warren Buffett once said that he prefers to get in on the next floor rather than the ground floor, that way he knows the elevator is working!

The main characteristic distinguishing small caps from larger caps is the possibility of getting a relative bargain on a fast-growing company, because the big buyers are not competing for shares yet. Thus, our selection criteria need to be broadened. As regards forward P/E relative to industry, we want stocks whose P/E is in the 50% to 100% range. The same is true for PEG and P/S. Stocks below 50% probably reflects the existence of misgivings on the part of other small-cap buyers. Needless to say, these numbers are not to be taken strictly.

Special Situations

Occasionally, you will notice a stock that has sudden appeal because of some event that suddenly increases the market for its product, or the stock is driven down for irrelevant reasons. That these are worth acting on is shown by the fact that the Value Line investment advisors have a small-cap special situations newsletter. (This may be available in a library near you. Check it out.) Two recent examples come to mind.

Immediately after the U.S. markets opened following the 11 September terrorist attacks, travel industry stocks dived. Looking at cruise ship companies, I saw that some companies such as Carnival lost half their value over about ten days. On checking their fundamentals, it was clear that P&O Princess (POC), which had dropped from $22 to $11, was a great short-term buy. By early November it was back up to $15. But then there was news that the company might be bought out and the stock soared to $23 by the new year. Having the nerve to buy at the bottom would have given one a 100% profit in 3½ months. The same events suddenly increased the demand for certain security products, causing their values to jump. Almost any catastrophic event provides opportunities, even in larger-cap stocks.

Another, different, sort of bargain arose because of alleged accounting misdemeanors at a company called Enterasys. The company announced on Friday, 1 Feb 02, that it was being investigated by the SEC. A company I was following, Riverstone Networks (RSTN), found its stock dropping 25% that day, so they felt it necessary to put out a press release on Saturday to make it clear that they were not being investigated by the SEC. Apparently some people thought that Riverstone was also being investigated. It may have been a guilt by association thing. Both companies were spinoffs from Cabletron. Despite their press release, RSTN opened almost $2 lower at $14 on the following Monday. Subsequently it dropped to $12. I bought some at $13.66, considerably lower than what I thought I would have to pay. The amazing thing about this sequence of events is that a brokerage firm announced an upgrade on the stock before the markets opened on Monday. As this case shows, there's no telling what kind of special situation might arise.

To spot special situation opportunities, monitor the investment news on "globeinvestor.com" and one or more of the U.S. investment sites. Personally, I like the Yahoo! "In Play" site. Most of these opportunities are for short-term gains, so you should treat them as separate from your core portfolio.

Evidence For An Impending Longer-Term Rise In Stock Price

The novice investor almost always responds incorrectly to news about stocks they are interested in. You should emulate the pros: "professionals eye the news in a peculiar way. They are prepared to learn from it, but they are not much intrigued by the literal content of a news story ... What interests pros is not the content of the news but the market's subsequent reaction to it. If the news about a specific company is bad, and it comes at the end of a long string of bad news, the market may not react at all ... an indication that everyone who might want to sell has already sold. Say the news is good – perhaps a stellar earnings report. In a climbing stock the normal pattern of price reaction would be a quick runup followed by a quick sell-off ... Canny investors eye the stock closely in the week following this knee-jerk buy/sell sequence. If the stock's normal uptrend does not emerge in the week or ten days following good, then it could well be that the pool of potential buyers is empty. This means the stock may have reached a major top ... *Instead of watching the for direct clues on whether to buy or sell, pros watch for the market's subsequent reaction or unreaction to news* " (Gianturco, p.39).

Generally, stock movements arising from company news are governed by the "law of unexpected results". That is, if the news is better than the pros expected, the stock rises; if it is worse than expected, the stock falls.

A variety of events can result in share value increasing. Almost all of the ones mentioned below generate an immediate rise, but the effects of some are only temporary, then the price falls back to where it was. Announcements of relatively big sales are often like that. On the other hand, some positive events have a longer-term effect, usually in conjunction with other such events. In general, any event that might lead you to believe that sales and/or earnings growth over the next few years will be greater than anticipated, will get reflected in a stock rise. Warning: you should wait a few days after these events before buying, because, as Gianturco points out, the price will spike up briefly, then fall back. If you buy on the day, you will almost certainly experience a loss in a few days. (Perhaps the warning should be "Caution! Day-traders at work.")

Major events that increase the likelihood of a longer-term share price increase, are the following:

(1) Analysts express enthusiasm for the company in the media. The major papers often report that a pro who buys or recommends stocks to funds or pension plans is keen on a stock. These opinions are generally based on a thorough analysis of the company and its

industry, so they can be taken as evidence of growth, which leads to longer-term increases in stock price.

(2) A shift in analyst buy-sell recommendations in a positive direction. Here we're referring to brokerage upgrades. An upgrade of an American or Canadian company from "hold" to "buy", or "buy" to "strong buy" by one of the major American brokerage firms will create immediate demand for a stock, but the change usually reflects a positive reappraisal of the company's growth.

(3) Announcement by a brokerage firm that it is beginning coverage of a company. This has about the same short term effect as an upgrade, if this is the first major firm to start covering the company. This sort of announcement amounts to a threshold crossing for a smaller company. It means that it is now "on the radar" for mutual fund and pension fund managers, so an acceleration of demand should occur.

(4) A firm revises its EPS estimates upwards for the current quarter and maybe the following quarter. Again, such changes reflect more optimism about sales and earnings growth, which bodes well for an increasing share price.

(5) Expressions of increased optimism about earnings prospects for the company's industry, in the media, by financial firm representatives. You will find such events occurring on ROB TV and CNBC, as well as in major business papers. This can cause demand for your stock as a member of the industry. When times are good for an industry, most of the better companies in it get to share in the prosperity. This is an example of the old adage, "A rising tide lifts all boats."

(6) Expressions of increased optimism for equity investing in general. Debates about whether to change portfolio weightings in bonds and stocks are about market sentiment. The adage of the previous paragraph applies, but note that some industries can be experiencing hard times even as the markets rise. In the late nineties, buying gold stocks would have been a mistake.

(7) The stock, at its present price, is relatively undervalued. Pro stock pickers are often asked to name stocks that are "bargains" or "undervalued" at present. Their willingness to name names

indicates that they believe there is such a thing as underpriced (and overpriced) stocks. Quite often, though, we don't get to hear what criteria they are using to make these valuation judgments.

Besides the foregoing news items specific to companies, there are also macro-economic ones that govern market sentiment, including consumer confidence, employment statistics, etc. Jeremy Siegel provides a nice compilation of the important ones in his Table 14-1 (Siegel p.199).

Portfolio Management

One of the biggest mistakes a novice investor can make is to begin by buying one or two stocks to gain experience. This pretty much guarantees that one's success or failure (more likely) is a matter of luck, good or bad. Psychological damage can occur regardless of outcome, especially if the investor is really lucky or really unlucky. In my case, the first stock I ever selected on my own quadrupled in value in a month or so. Was I lucky in my stock picking? Yes and no. I chose the stock conscientiously, so it wasn't blind luck that I bought it. The luck came in my timing. I bought just before it made a run, but I had little basis for buying then.

The psychological danger of such first time success is, of course, that one is apt to infer that stock picking is easy. This conviction, in turn, leads to a lack of caution which sets us up to make stupid mistakes. In stock picking a stupid mistake is, by definition, one that costs us good money. (I sometimes tell people that I like the stock market "game" because of the way we keep score!)

The converse of good luck is obvious, and is more likely what the novice investor will experience if she/he starts off buying a single stock. But in a way the first time loser comes out ahead of the first time winner: they get some education and, if they are lucky, go away thinking that stock picking isn't easy. A cautious approach is worth a lot in this "game". The downside in having a bad experience first time out is that one becomes so intimidated that one gives up on buying stocks altogether. This would be unfortunate if one has the psychological makeup to do well in the market.

How many stocks should one carry in one's main portfolio? Traditionally, it is held that more stocks, if properly selected, can lead to lower volatility in portfolio value. Modern portfolio theory has used mathematical tools to work out a precise answer. Here I will present the nice discussion of the topic found in Burton Malkiel's *A Random Walk Down Wall Street*.

Malkiel begins by distinguishing systematic risk and unsystematic risk: "systematic risk ... arises from the basic variability of stock prices in general and the tendency for all stocks to go along with the general market, at least to some extent. The remaining variability in a stock's returns is called unsystematic risk and results from factors peculiar to that particular company ..." (p.229).

Systematic risk is commonly expressed by the parameter "beta": "The beta calculation is essentially a comparison between the movements of an individual stock (or portfolio) and the movements of the market as a whole" (p.229). This is commonly done using the S&P 500 index or the TSE 300. A beta of 1 says that a stock has the same variability as the index. Thus, a TSE stock with a beta of 1.59, is 59% more variable than the TSE 300. If the index rises 10%, the stock will (on average) rise 15.9%. If a stock has a beta less than one, its swings are less wide than the index. These are considered more conservative stocks. Some stocks have negative betas, meaning they swing in the opposite direction to the market. Gold stocks are the best example.

As Malkiel points out, diversification can reduce unsystematic risk, but systematic risk, a large component of total variability, cannot be reduced by diversification: "It is precisely because all stocks move more or less in tandem ... that even diversified stock portfolios are risky" (p.230). Diversification can be used to pretty much eliminate unsystematic risk, though. How many stocks need to be held to do this? "Suppose we randomly select securities for our portfolio that tend on average to be just as volatile as the market ... as we add more and more securities the total risk of our portfolio declines ... When 10 securities are selected for our portfolio, a good deal of the unsystematic risk is eliminated ... by the time 20 well diversified securities are in the portfolio, the unsystematic risk is substantially eliminated and our portfolio (with a beta of 1) will tend to move up and down essentially in tandem with the market" (p.230).

Modern portfolio theorists have discovered that we can have the virtues of diversification with fewer stocks by holding complementary stocks. Apparently if these stocks are carefully selected to yield a collectively steady return throughout all phases of the economic cycle, as few as ten stocks can provide the desired effect. The ideal is to always have a stock in a declining sector matched by one in a rising sector. This mathematical possibility is what prompts *Investment Reporter* to advise holding stocks in all the sectors. For example, integrated oil companies (Exxon, Shell, etc.) do well in the first half of an economic contraction, but not so well in the later half. On the other hand, supermarket chains (including Loblaw's and Sobey's in Canada) do poorly in the first half, but well in the second half. (Stovall 1995, p.13) So to get a steady return through a market cycle you could begin by buying equal dollar amounts of Exxon and Loblaw's, perhaps. This advice is clearly assuming that the investor wants to follow a buy-and-hold approach, or, as the pros call it, a "long-term" approach. We might wonder why it might not be better to buy Exxon on the downturn, then switch to Loblaw's or Winn-Dixie or A&P as the economy starts to improve. This should give us the best of both worlds. Of course, getting the timing right would require a higher level of involvement with our portfolio than the pros assume we want, and they would probably say that amateurs are no good at market timing.

The problem with this approach is that it will probably not be possible to find 10 to 20 stocks that are individually high-growth and that complement each other in the right way. It would be difficult to find *any* high-growth companies in some sectors. If we go for high growth companies we will probably end up with a high proportion of stocks from only a few sectors, such as technology.

This would, of course, increase the volatility of the portfolio, since most of one's stocks will rise and fall together.

The stress on diversification by traditional thinkers is a byproduct of a buy-and-hold philosophy. Overall portfolio safety is a matter of reducing overall volatility. If one is not prepared to sell stocks that go down significantly (but temporarily?), one better have other stocks that are going up to offset the dropping ones. But if we use the TrendPoint! strategy we do not have to take steps to offset falling stocks. We just sell them at their SP. Under this system it is not crucial to select stocks with a view to diversification. Of course, a portfolio of 10 to 20 stocks will reduce unsystematic risk to some degree anyway. One is not likely to end up with nothing but wireless service providers, for example. So if we make diversification a minor criterion for selection, how many stocks should we have in our portfolio? One writer advocates ten: "I recommend to my clients that they build up to a maximum of ten quality core stocks ..." (Schott p.40).

I have already argued that the worst way to get started in stock investing is to buy one or two stocks and see how it goes. The best beginner approach is to gain some investing knowledge, do some stock research, then create a portfolio of five to ten stocks. Buy them all at one time! Instead of putting your $10,000 into one or two stocks, put $2000 each in five, or even $1000 each in ten. In the first scenario, if one loses half its value overnight (a real possibility in the present market climate) your portfolio has dropped 10% in value. In the second scenario it will have fallen only 5%. To retain your composure in either of these scenarios it is imperative that you focus on the "big picture", the total portfolio value. If you "stew" about the 50% loss in the one stock you will simply have to train yourself not to. Otherwise, you will find that, even if you make money with your astutely selected portfolio, you will suffer just like you would if your "portfolio" consisted of only one stock. I'm not suggesting you should *overlook* 50% drops, indeed, part of the purpose of this book is to show you how to avoid such a grisly situation. But as those active in the market in the past few years will attest, such a drop can indeed happen overnight. All it takes is a company whose stock is at a high valuation to report that it is seriously missing its EPS estimate, or says anything that suggests accounting irregularities may have occurred, or that it is being sued for patent infringement.

For do-it-yourself investors the main constraint on portfolio management is time availability. In general, the amount of time spent in managing a portfolio should be proportional to the number of stocks held. You should begin by frankly acknowledging how much time you can *realistically* make available for maintaining your portfolios. If you are already doing some independent research and market following, and have had some success, you may appreciate that these activities can be addictive. If you are inclined to this addiction, I suggest you set aside a definite time slot for your investing activities, and stick to it. If you have a spouse, tell him/her what that time slot is, so they can help you comply with your time allotment by nagging you if you don't!

Supervision of the price movements of your stocks is easy with the internet resources we now have. This data can be checked after the market closes every day. Monitoring portfolios is easier these days because you can set up integrated portfolios using Quicken or one of the other software packages, or just put them on your personal page on websites such as the one operated by *The Globe & Mail*. Web brokerage sites such as E*Trade are also good . The former is free, the latter are made available if you have a brokerage account. Canada Stockwatch charges $5 per month for minimal service, but offers several extra useful features. If a stock has set a new high, adjust your SP value based on the SP% you are using for that stock. Same for any mutual funds. If a stock on your watch list has hit a new low, adjust your BP based on the BP% you have chosen for the stock. This takes little time, it can be done daily.

Most of the time allotted to investments involves research for buying decisions, which includes following market trends as reported on TV and on websites. Theoretically, the approach I advocate does not require following the news (other than share price) from and about the companies whose stocks one owns. Indeed, doing so can interfere with one's sell decisions. The only occasion on which you need to review the news about your company is when it is the weakest (in turns of price performance) of your holdings. The need to do so then will be explained below.

You might be thinking that not following the news of your stocks takes some of the fun out of investing. After all, we all like to see our selection acumen vindicated. Whether or not you read company news after you have the stock is a personal matter, in the sense that each of us needs to decide whether or not doing so interferes with our selling. Personally, I am better able to sell at my SP without letting company news influence me than I used to be. So now I do read the news about my stocks. But there was a time when I did let it interfere with selling. Then again, I'm the sort of person who feels more comfortable knowing why things are happening. Most people who have regular jobs can probably effectively own a maximum of about 20 stocks, but unless you are very experienced I think 10 is a good number. This gives some diversification. Another consideration is efficiency in trading costs. You can buy and sell more easily, and at a better price if you trade in lots of 100 shares, at least. Since the median share price for TSE companies with market caps of at least $250 million is about $30, you would have about $3000 invested in each stock. $30,000 would get you a 10-stock portfolio. If you have less than this to invest you can go with fewer stocks, or smaller numbers of shares. To get some diversification you should have at least five stocks.

Beyond having at least five, it is not crucial how many stocks you hold. You might find you can manage 20, or maybe you will be more comfortable with 5. But there is something to be said for deciding on an upper limit and sticking with it. This helps you in your decision making in the following way. Suppose you decide on a limit of 10. The market is bullish and you find yourself at some point with 10. A new one on your watch list (see below) seems a timely buy. Should you add it? If this was the last one during the current bull run that you would want to add, maybe you should. But others may later beg for inclusion, so do you add them too? First thing you know, you might have a bigger portfolio than you can handle. Thus, it's better to pick a limit and stick to it.

If you do this you can use the following buy and sell strategy. What if you want to add a new pick and your chosen limit is 10 and you already have 10? Well, you identify the one of the 10 that seems to have the worst prospects for price growth, and compare it with the candidate. If the latter seems to have superior potential, you sell the one and buy the other. Following this approach, you always have the stocks with what you regard as the best return potential in your portfolio. The Motley Fool guys say: "If you have a ten-stock portfolio, don't look at it as a series of ten separate, difficult decisions about when to sell. No! Look at it as a single investment portfolio to which you'll want to *add* new stocks when the time arises. *When the time arises, you can make room for that exciting new opportunity by shedding whichever of your holdings looks to be the most fully valued i.e., appears to have the least room for more near-term appreciation*" (D.&T. Gardner, p. 183).

We might call this the "Glen Sather" approach. During the great years of the Edmonton Oilers hockey team, it was rumored that some of the players noticed that Sather traded people at season's end regardless of how successful the season was. It seemed to them that Sather usually traded the player who seemed to contribute least. It didn't matter how much this player contributed, if he was ranked lowest by Sather, he was gone. This "nobody is safe" feeling was no doubt very motivating! Another sports analogy comes from Earl Weaver, the manager of the Baltimore Orioles in their great years. When a player was doing more bench time than he liked and complained to Weaver, Weaver would tell him "Make me play you." The idea was for the player to work harder than the starting person at his position, and perform well enough when he got in the lineup to force Weaver to play him every day. We can think of our stock buys the same way. When the best watch list candidate starts to look better than the poorest performer in the portfolio, make a switch. In doing this there may be feelings of regret to deal with, though.

How much turnover you get is a function of the criteria you use for stock picking, and the bullishness of the market. If a bear market is being experienced, you may well have fewer than your limit, and if things are really bad, you may have an empty portfolio. All your stocks may have fallen to their sell points and none on your watch list has risen to their BP. (I do not support the concept of portfolio relativity, which dictates that you should always have your portfolio full of stocks whose companies have the best earnings prospects, regardless of their price performance. To be ready to take advantage of good buys, it is better to be out of a falling market. Using the TrendPoint! strategy, you buy these good prospects only when their prices have risen to the BP you have assigned to them.)

Watch List

A watch list consists of companies with fundamentals that imply that they are likely to grow their sales and earnings at a relatively high rate *and* whose share price you expect to increase accordingly. All the stocks on the list should be ones you believe have the potential to provide a good capital return, but they can still be divided into two kinds. One kind will be those that are eligible to be bought because their price is above the BP value (up BP% from the last low) and above the SP value derived from your assigned SP%. These will be ones that you judge to have less return potential than the one you own that has the lowest potential.

The other kind is those that are ineligible because they are below the BP value needed to qualify for purchase. These will include stocks you have previously owned but have had to be sold because they fell below their SP value. These will be companies whose fundamentals are unchanged, or still good enough to warrant purchasing when they rise to the BP. Since the TrendPoint! selling strategy is purely technical, it can be a serious mistake to sell a stock and ignore it after that. This would be appropriate if we were following a "hold until fundamentals change negatively" strategy, but in my system you sell regardless of how good company prospects are. And you can buy back when the stock resumes its positive momentum, providing the fundamentals still warrant it. This gives us a chance to add shares after a decline caused by bear market conditions, as illustrated earlier. In 1999, during its big runup, I must have bought and sold Nortel six or eight times, gaining a bit each time. In retrospect, I probably used a SP% that was too small. But I never dropped Nortel from my watch list because its fundamentals were improving all the time.

A significant advantage to this buy-sell-rebuy approach is that it reduces research effort. Rebuying the stock does not require researching it from scratch. In fact, you can be more comfortable with your holdings if they are long-term interests. Remember, in this trading system, having sold a stock is no reason not to buy it, because you might have sold it because of a market drop rather than any problem with the company.

<u>Due Diligence</u>

Since most of the time is spent gathering information leading to buy decisions, how much time you need to put in depends on how much due diligence you need to do to feel comfortable and get good results. Using the TrendPoint! approach means that one need not do as much research as a buy-and-hold approach would require. It's like comparing a date with a marriage. One can invite someone on a date without a lot of investigation into details about them. If things don't "click" we can break off the relationship without a lot of angst and suffering. If things do click, and we're thinking about marriage, we need to know almost everything important about the other person. Real due diligence is required! The same contrast applies to stocks. If your practice is to hold stocks for years, then you need to investigate the company thoroughly. Since the pros recommend this long-term attitude, it is not surprising that they recommend a lot of financial analysis before buying. But most amateurs are not knowledgeable enough to evaluate the data reliably. Does a company have a lot of debt? What counts as a "lot" in their business? In software companies, any debt is a negative, since most companies can finance expansion by floating more stock. On the other hand, an electric utility may have a lot in dollar value, but not relative to the industry.

The important point here is that *what the stock analysts think is what is important*. Their judgments influence share price because their money managers buy and sell based on their recommendations. If your personal analysis leads to a judgment different from theirs you will find yourself "fighting the tape".

Every investor should do enough analysis of companies whose stock they might purchase to feel comfortable with a buy decision. This is a purely psychological guideline for due diligence, and as such, it is subjective – up to a point. What might make you feel comfortable with your decision might be rather more than I need to do to get the same level of comfort. At a minimum, everyone needs to check out the EPS estimates for the current year and the following year, or the revenue estimates, preferably, to establish that company growth is adequate. The best source for Canadian EPS estimates that I have found is *Investor's Digest*, which publishes data every second issue. For U.S. listed companies the data is easily found at "http://quote.yahoo.com".

The most useful information on company prospects is contained in analyst reports from the bigger brokerage houses and banks, but in Canada these are not commonly available free, except to customers. For bigger U.S. companies and Canadian ones listed in the U.S. they can be bought from Zack's website. Since they are expensive, it is best to read the abstract before buying. A better source is probably Morningstar, which, for $90U.S. per year will give you access to their independent analyst reports. Another good source is Value Line, but it is very expensive. For large-cap American companies you might find their reports in your public library, or a university library. Value Line is highly respected as an independent source.

Just to keep optimism under control it is advisable to read the "disclosure of risks" section of the last quarterly report. For companies listed in Canada, reports can be found at "www.sedar.com" For American ones see "www.freeedgar". The "disclosure of risks" section usually identifies the company's competitors, so you can do some meaningful comparisons.

I do not think it necessary to delve into the actual financial reports other than to check the sales and earnings figures, and in some cases the "cash flow from operations". The reports have been scrutinized thoroughly by the analysts, who have a lot more expertise at this than most of us. It is more efficient and reliable to rely on their reports, if available. If not, I take their EPS estimates to reflect their judgment of company financial condition and prospects. Second-hand opinion from an expert is generally more reliable than one's own first-hand opinion. But as I said, one product of due diligence is being comfortable with one's selections.

If you have to delve into financial report details to feel you have done your homework, then do. But a word of warning: there is such a thing as doing too much research on a company. The more you do, the more ego involvement you may have, so if you buy the stock you may have trouble selling in a timely fashion. When a drop in the share price is not obviously due to overall market sentiment, selling will feel like admitting a mistake, and after doing a lot of research we may be victims of our own tendency to rationalize the downturn and hang on. The same can happen if you have owned a stock for a long time.

There are various sources for finding promising companies. The most efficient way is to use one of the screening programs found at investor websites such as globeinvestor.com for TSE companies or Yahoo! for U.S. stocks. Besides these superior sources, the print and TV media these days do a much better job of providing stock investors with analysis, forecasts and suggested stock picks. Professional stock pickers are interviewed on "ROB TV" and on daily and weekly U.S. investment programs. The *Globe & Mail* and the *National Post* are the best dailies for Canadian investment information, and of course the *Wall Street Journal* and *Investor's Business Daily* are the best U.S. sources. *Barron's* is a prestigious weekly. In Canada *Investor's Digest*, is published in Toronto twice a month. A subscription costs about $140 per year. You may be able to find it in your local library. *Canadian Business* is a useful source of leads for companies based in Canada.

You need to do some independent investigation before buying any stock recommended in the media. The person making the recommendation may be using different selection criteria than you are. They may be running a value fund, so that the stock they name may not have the revenue growth rate you want to see.

You should spend a few hours a week looking for new stock ideas, and researching the most promising ones. Part of this should be watching a few TV shows that bring professionals on to elicit recommendations. I especially like Lou Rukeyser's show, formerly on PBS, now on CNBC. Of course, if you have the time you can get more ideas from CNBC (All stocks, all the time! During the day, anyway.) The Canadian counterpart is ROB TV. If you can fit it in, it can be helpful to catch these channels before the markets open.

CHAPTER FOUR

MUTUAL FUNDS

Generally speaking the appeal of mutual funds lies in their inherent diversification, which makes them less volatile than individual stocks. The approach to funds that I advocate is to trade them like individual stocks, to the extent possible. This is not always possible because some funds impose a penalty for withdrawing your money within a period of time after purchase. A common period is three months. And, of course, many funds have load fees. The best way to operate your mutual fund portfolio is to have it with one of the big banks if you are Canadian, or E*Trade and its competitors. They do not charge anything for moving your money from one of their funds to another. But the banks do not enable you to buy all Canadian funds, whereas E*Trade and its competitors do.

Comparing Fund Types

For people who lack the time to identify promising stocks, funds are better. There are a limited number of them that will appear attractive at any particular time. And if one adopts TrendPoint!, volatility is not an issue with funds, because they do not reverse themselves quickly. This being so, to maximize our return we ought to concentrate on the funds that will provide the highest returns over time. One valid clue to identifying the types of funds that will have the best returns is to look at the past of the more popular fund categories. On the next page I present a table based on the 15 year record up to the end of 2001, indicating the APR (annualized percentage return), the amount that an initial investment of $1000 would have become after 15 years (less in a few important cases), plus the highest annual return and lowest annual return to give some idea of comparative volatility, and the number of years with a return above 20%. The real return is "APR" less 2.5%, the average inflation rate over the period.

TABLE: FUND PERFORMANCE

CATEGORY	15 YR APR	ACCUM	HIGHEST RETURN	LOWEST RETURN	YRS > 20%
Cdn Equity	8.74%	$3510	29.8%	- 11.5%	3
Cdn Balanced	7.71%	$3050	16.5%	- 2.4%	3
Cdn Dividend	9.32%	$3810	23.8%	- 4.4%	3
U.S. Equity	10.7%	$4590	29.7%	- 10.2%	5
Cdn Small Cap	8.8%	$3550	40.9%	- 13.9%	1
U.S. Sm & Mid	15.65%	$8850	43.8%	- 6.2%	8
Precious Metals	3.8%	$1750	96.2%	- 41.0%	4
Natural Resources	10.0%	$4180	78.3%	- 30.0%	4
Sci & Tech (8 yrs)	14.5%	$2950	100.7%	- 34.9%	4
Health Care (9 yrs)	17.8%	$4370	33.1%	- 10.2%	3
Cdn Bond	8.2%	$3240	19.1%	- 5.8%	0
Cdn Money Mkt	6.2%	$2450	12.5%	+ 2.4%	0

Source: *Globe & Mail*

The strategy I advocate is a fairly aggressive one, but not high risk because it uses TrendPoint!. What we seek to do is to buy a fund at its BP, then sell when it comes down to its SP. You will find that, compared to stocks, funds have a lower SP% because of the diversification resulting from holding 50 to 100 stocks.

The main problem in achieving this goal of timely buying and selling is how to monitor the sector. One approach that is fairly efficient is to pick a top performer in each sector that offers an occasional opportunity for a good gain. This is likely to be found in sectors whose companies have prospects of high future EPS growth. Earlier we identified two such, science & technology and health care. Besides these, the "U.S. Small and Mid-Cap" category catches the eye because of its high median return (15.65%) and the 8 years out of 15 in which the category made returns of over 20%. But the better ones are load funds and must be held as foreign content in Canadian RRSP's. Also, the "U.S. Equity" category has done well, better than its Canadian counterpart, providing five years in which returns exceeded 20%. However, these funds contain mostly slow growth large companies, so high returns are not to be expected.

Having identified these sectors as the most attractive ones, we can proceed to choose a fund that we take to be the best performer over the last few years, say. Canadians should choose an RRSP-eligible one if our money is tax-sheltered, but if there isn't one that seems good enough, we can pick one that can be held as "foreign content". (30% of an RRSP portfolio amount can be in this category.) We should also pick a no-load one, since we may not be buying for the long term.

In the "Science & Technology" category I like "Altamira Science & Technology". As of early 2002, it is the best-performing Science & Technology fund over both three and five year periods. It is a no-load fund, but qualifies only as foreign content for Canadian RRSP's. However, this does not represent an obstacle because Altamira has recently created an RRSP-eligible tracking fund that matches the returns of the original. It is called "Altamira

RSP Science & Technology". So we can now, in effect, hold this fund as Canadian content.

American investors, of course, have a greater variety of choices. This is where the Morningstar mutual fund website really becomes useful. Screening for technology funds at this time I see that the Fidelity Select funds are still near the top after many years.

In using TrendPoint! to trade funds we need to remember that they are valued only at the end of the trading day, unless they are Exchange Traded Funds. This means that when the fund falls below our SP, we sell the following day. Because of this, it can happen that we sell at a value above or below our SP. When we put in our sell order on the day following, we cannot know that this will happen, although if we see that tech stocks are doing well we may expect to sell at a slightly higher price. Should we hold on when it looks like this may happen? I do not advise it. Second-guessing our decisions sooner or later leads to ignoring them.

The Altamira Science & Technology Fund opened in the spring of 1998. It moved up nicely until it reached an "inflection point" on 21 Oct 99, after which there was an acceleration of return because the NASDAQ tech bubble had started to expand. Let's see what would happen if we determine an SP% based on the interval between the fund's starting date and 21 Oct 99. The figure I find to be optimum is 12%. Buying on 21 Oct 99, we get the following transactions up to 26 Feb 02:

```
21 Oct 99    Buy 100 @ $19.38 (Portfolio Total = $1938)
16 Mar 00    Sell @ $47.70 (Portfolio Value = $4770)
19 Apr 00    Buy @ $37.74 (126.39 shares)
11 May 00    Sell @ $36.58 (Portfolio Value = $4623)
02 Jun 00    Buy @ $41.36 (111.77 shares)
28 Jul 00    Sell @ $41.31 (Portfolio Value = $4617)
18 Aug 00    Buy @ $47.55 (97.10 shares)
04 Oct 00    Sell @ $45.97 (Portfolio Value = $4464)
17 Oct 00    Buy @ $44.80 (99.64 shares)
26 Oct 00    Sell @ $41.15 (Portfolio Value = $4100)
06 Nov 00    Buy @ $43.45 (94.36 shares)
```

13 Nov 00   Sell @ $36.80 (Portfolio Value = $3472)
06 Dec 00   Buy @ $35.36 (98.19 shares)
15 Dec 00   Sell @ $33.65 (Portfolio Value = $3304)
29 Dec 00   Buy @ $28.87 (114.44 shares)
03 Jan 01   Sell @ $29.59 (Portfolio Value = $3382)
15 Jan 01   Buy @ $30.26 (111.76 shares)
05 Feb 01   Sell @ $30.16 (Portfolio Value = $3371)
11 Apr 01   Buy @ $18.67 (180.56 shares)
31 May 01   Sell @ $20.18 (Portfolio Value = $3644)
11 Oct 01   Buy @ $12.86 (283.36 shares)
05 Feb 02   Sell @ $14.06 (Portfolio Value = $3984)
26 Feb 02   End date. Stock price = $13.37.

Portfolio Value = $3984. Return = +105.6%, APR = 35.93%.
Buy & Hold Return = -31.0%, APR = -14.6%.

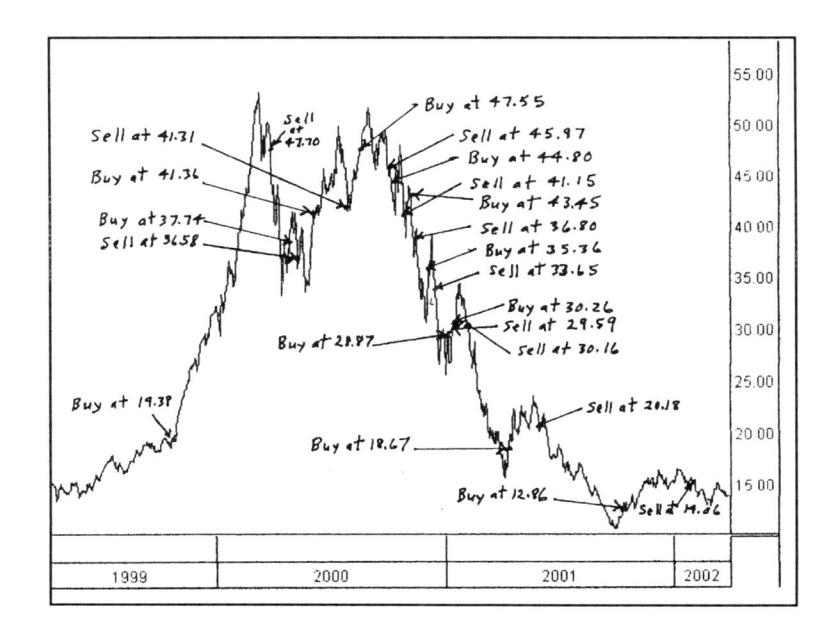

This excellent result required 22 trades over 28 months. If I were to have actually made these transactions through my bank brokerage account, I would have paid out $40 each time I sold (no charge for buying), for a total of $440. The net return, then, is based on the ratio (3984 - 440)/1938, so it is 82.9% (APR = 29.2%). But since the $40 is a flat rate, if I had started with an investment ten times as large (i.e., $19,380), the net return would have been derived from the ratio (39,840 - 440)/19,380, which works out to 103.3%. (APR = 35.2%)

If you think that this is a lot of trading, relatively speaking it is, because 2000 was easily the most volatile year this fund ever had. This is reflected in the 14 trades that would have been executed, versus 6 for 2001. Note also that between 31 May 01 and 11 Oct 01 we would have been out of the fund, a four month break in which the buy & hold people would have seen their holding lose 36% of its value. Again, although TrendPoint! involves trading, this would not be as stressful as the buy & hold approach. A large number of investors suffered losses of this magnitude when the tech bubble burst. By contrast, the TrendPoint! user would have done very well indeed. Most investors would probably have been happy to get away without a major loss after the tech bubble burst, but TrendPoint! would have enabled us to actually take advantage of the bubble by ensuring timely buying and selling.

On reviewing all these transactions, you might conclude that anyone who went through all this must be overly dedicated to this particular fund. Why keep buying back in as the NAV keeps dropping? First of all, if you feel compelled to ask this, it is almost certain that you are relying on knowledge of where the NAV was going, not just on where it had been. Would we know at any particular closing value that the price would not recover? In mid-April the NAV had fallen to 35.00. Did we know it was heading back to 50.00 in early September? No. But this persistence in buying back would be rational only in late 2000 if we believed that the odds favored a recovery. But that would probably not be the view of anyone following events. Tech companies were lowering their EPS guidance numbers all over the place. The wise

TrendPoint! user would probably have chosen not to buy back, at some point, in late October or early November.

One way of dealing with the issue of knowing when to stop is to invoke the rule I suggested earlier: do not buy when the NASDAQ Composite Index falls below its 200-day simple moving average. This index is closely correlated with the fund. If we had followed this extra rule our net return for the period would have been +127%, rather than 82.9%. There would have been only 12 trades made, because the Index was below its 200-day moving average for about four months in late 2000. If we had started with 1000 shares instead of 100, the net return would have been +138%. So the index constraint concept seems to warrant adoption.

This is not a specially selected example intended to show the superiority of TrendPoint! for investing in funds. Many people moved their money into the high tech sector in 1999 when the bubble started to grow. Unless they invested in early 1999, they will have losses to live with.

You might argue that there is some "rear view mirror" investment decisions involved in selecting this particular fund, but in fact each of the other three science and technology funds that had established track records in late 1999 had comparable return profiles since then. So it would not have mattered much which one I had picked as an example.

Using the 12% SP/BP, then, one can trade the fund over extended periods, being confident that over the longer term that it will go up. But as of 01 Mar 02 I am out of the fund, waiting for a bottom and a 12% trend reversal.

The next category that I would be engaged with is "Health Care". It is the other sector distinguished by prospects of good EPS growth in the foreseeable future. (You may recall that, earlier, on screening for high-growth stocks on Morningstar, most of the ones identified were in these two categories.) Most of the funds are relatively new. By virtue of its returns, the "Talvest Global Health Care RSP" fund must be preferred by Canadians, even though it is a load fund. It's non-RRSP original has by far the best three and five-year returns in its sector. On examining the price movements of the fund, I conclude that an SP/BP% of 5 % is appropriate, but I will not give the details as I did for the previous fund. With this value, trading between 13 Jun 00 (it's first day of trading) and 12 Jun 01, involves five trades and gives a gross return of 29.8% (versus 25% for buy-and-hold).

In addition to these two top performers you should screen the whole universe of funds to find candidates that do not concentrate on high tech and health care. Using "globefund.com" right now I find that, even at the bottom of a bear market there are at least 50 Canadian funds with three-year returns of above 10% per year. Most of these are resource, energy, or small-cap funds, but they can provide a good return while we are out of our other funds.

As is evident from the foregoing, using TrendPoint! to enhance or protect returns involves "adopting" suitable funds, in the sense that over a long period of time one buys and sells the same carefully selected ones, instead of jumping around within a sector. It is not necessary to invest simultaneously in more than three or four funds, even if you buy only sector funds. Using TrendPoint! will protect you when a sector turns down.

Index Funds

Index funds have really become popular in recent years as a result, perhaps, of the success of the Vanguard funds in the U.S. That company pioneered the concept with their S&P 500 index fund that tracks the S&P 500 index. Part of the attractiveness of index funds is that they are passively managed. The manager simply buys stocks, in the correct proportion, that become included in the index, and sells those that are dropped. No independent decisions are needed, so no expensive analysts need be hired. This allows the funds to charge a much lower management expense fee. Another factor in making index funds attractive was the public becoming aware that the performance of actively managed funds was judged in terms of index performance: the S&P 500 in the U.S. and the TSE 300 in Canada. When people found out that less than half of the actively managed funds did as well in a given year as the indexes, investors reached the obvious conclusion: why buy an actively managed fund that has more than a 50% chance of underperforming the index when one can, in effect, buy the index itself -- cheaper?

A cautionary note must be sounded in regard to Canadian index funds based on the TSE 300 and the S&P/TSE 60. The membership in these is determined by market capitalization, and since we do not have as many really large-cap companies in Canada, the ones that are largest can represent unduly high proportions of the total index. This is what happened during the high tech bubble of 2000. Nortel and JDS Uniphase were by far the largest companies on the TSE. At one point it was estimated that Nortel represented more than 30% of the TSE 300 capitalization. So when it fell from a high of $122 on 01 Sep 00 to under $15 in mid-2001, the TSE 300 fell 30%. Many Canadians were hurt by this because their investment advisors had convinced them to put their RRSP money in Canadian index funds. But part of the rationale for this, protective diversification, did not apply in 2000, as many people found to their chagrin. Since then the TSE has created a new index called the "TSE 300 Capped Index" which "limits the exposure to any one company to less than 10%".

The best way for Canadians to avoid such an outcome in buying index funds is to buy ones that track U.S. stocks. In the U.S. no single company, including GE, can rise to a dominant position in the S&P 500. Each of the big banks has a fund that tracks the S&P 500, and so does Altamira. These also have the advantage of paying a higher return (see the returns table given earlier). You need to appreciate, though, that even using TrendPoint!, you cannot get high returns this way. A lot of the companies in the S&P 500 are slow growth ones, relative to the ones in the NASDAQ 100. Three banks, BMO, CIBC, and TD have RSP Index funds that track the NASDAQ 100, so if science and technology, or health care funds are too "frisky" for you, you might consider one of these. But be warned: just as for the sector funds, you can only do well with these if you use TrendPoint! or some other system that includes a selling principle. They are too volatile for buy-and-hold. On the other hand, if you do use TrendPoint! in trading these, you will earn relatively higher returns.

Exchange Traded Funds (ETF's)

Lately a new type of quasi-fund has become available. This is the "Exchange Traded Fund". The TSE has "XIU", which tracks the S&P/TSE60. They call this an "index participation fund". The main advantage of such tracking stocks is that the management fee is very low, and (very important in volatile markets) you can buy or sell at any time during trading hours. In the U.S. the American Stock Exchange (AMEX) has created a variety of these based on the various indexes used to measure stock market performance. You can even buy ones called "SPDR's" that track industry sectors. See the NASDAQ website for details, but Canadians should note that these can be held only in RRSP's as foreign content. XIU, of course, qualifies as Canadian content. There is even a Canadian technology ETF, "XIT". It is relatively volatile, but with an SP% of 10%, trading it from its first major bottom on 04 Apr 01 up to 28 Feb 02 would give a gross return of 24.9%. This would involve 14 trades, so to get a good net return you would have needed to start with 1000 shares at $9.12. Again, buying at this price would give you a loss over the period if you bought and held.

Chase Hot Funds?

Inspection of the relationship between fund assets and performance shows that the public is more apt to put money in a fund if it is outperforming the market. (This was behind the choices I made earlier.) An obvious example from recent years is the AIC Advantage fund sold in Canada. As it began achieving big returns, the money poured in. For the years 1995 through 1997, the APR was an incredible 46.1%! Is there merit in putting money in when a fund is delivering big returns? The professionals argue that this strategy does not work.

In the 27 Jan 97 of *MacLean's*, the annual mutual fund issue, they conveniently supplied a list of the top 10 funds of 1996, ranked by NAV (Net Asset Value) increase, with the top fund increasing 89.1% and number 10 increasing 52.8%. This comment is provided: "Impressive numbers, to be sure. But that is no reason to rush out and buy them, cautions Rob Heinkel, a professor of finance at the University of British Columbia. "Basing your investment decisions on one year's performance is dangerous at best," he says. In one year almost anything can happen." Adds Richard Croft, co-author of *The Fundline Advisor*: "In many cases, last year's winners may turn out to be this year's average players."

Then the year 2000 mutual fund issue came out. Because 1999 was a good year for Canadian large-cap funds and index funds because of Nortel, BCE, JDS Uniphase, and a few other tech stocks, there was some wavering about the conventional approach. Again, though, we found a familiar refrain: "... experts caution that a fund's history is no guarantee of future performance. By definition, a fund manager who produces returns above the market average must be doing something that his or her peers are not - but this year's formula for success could easily turn into next year's recipe for disaster." (p.19)

This advice and the rationales for it can be found in financial advice columns throughout the land. The *MacLean's* article is just one more example of what can only be called the conventional wisdom. The funds themselves support it indirectly by, quite responsibly, reminding us in their prospectuses that past performance does not guarantee future success. Some, such as Altamira, even go so far as to say that "Past performance of mutual funds are not indicative of future performance." Do they mean that past performance is *no* evidence of future performance?

There is something fishy about this kind of disclaimer. In most areas of complex human endeavour we take previous success to be, not only *some* evidence, but *good* evidence of future success. Why is it different in fund picking?

How might we confirm or refute the conventional wisdom? An obvious test would be to try an extreme version of relying on past performance: see what happens if we hold only one Canadian large-cap fund, which is bought at the start of the calendar year. The fund we buy is the one with the best return for the last calendar year. I made such a study using the ten-year period from 01 Jan 90 to 01 Jan 00, relying on the data contained in the *Globe & Mail*, "15-Year Mutual Fund Review", 03 Feb 00 issue. The results are interesting.

The gross APR return (ignoring sales commissions) was 12.3%. Deducting an MER of 2.4%, the median value, gave a net APR of 9.9%. This contrasts favorably with a gross median APR return for the category of 8.9% and net APR of 6.5%. The difference is bigger than it looks expressed in APR's. If you had invested $10,000 initially, the first approach would have given a net profit of $15,700. The median net profit for the category would have been $8,800. Both of these sets ignore sales commissions, which are difficult to quantify. However, it is interesting that, if we had used the best-last-year strategy but bought only no-load funds, the net APR would have been higher: 10.3%. In this version the net profit on a $10,000 investment would have been $16,650.

You might suspect that this higher return involved greater volatility, but you would be wrong. In fact, using this strategy over the 10 years, our "portfolio" that bought both load and no-load funds had two losing year (1990 and 1994). It lost 6.6% (9.0% including MER fee) in 1990 and 11.5% in 1994 (13.9% including MER). The median fund would have experienced three losing years (1990, 1994, and 1998). It would have lost 12.2% (14.4% including MER) in 1990, 2.6% (5.0% including MER) in 1994), and 1.7% in 1998 (4.1% including MER). The no-load version also had two losing years, the same two. In 1990 the loss was 6.6% (9.0% including MER), and 7.8% in 1994 (10.2% including MER).

In the 2000 issue *MacLean's* advocated using a previous three-years criterion to reduce losses due to mistiming. Does this work any better than the one-year criterion? Looking back ten years, as before, the gross APR was 7.4% (versus 12.31% for the one-year version), net 5.0% (versus 9.9%). This three-year version gives a result lower than the median too. And there were three losing years. So, contrary to their view, buying the best performer over the last three years gives a *worse* result than using only the last year.

Does this buy-last-year's-best strategy seem too good to be true? One source of skepticism was reflected in a comment I quoted from *MacLean's*: "In many cases, last year's winners may turn out to be this year's average players." The idea here has valid application in many competitive pursuits. For example, there is the common phenomenon of the ball player who has an unexpected "career year". He hits 20 points above his normal average, then regresses the next year. Statisticians call this regression to the mean.

The reason why the one-year strategy works is that regression does not fully occur in the year following the "career year", i.e., the year in which a fund has the top return. Following the purchase, only five of ten actually bettered their previous-year return. But in seven cases, the return still exceeded the median return of the group. So the principle seems to be that if the last-year return is high enough, the following year's return will be above average, even if usually lower than its previous year. To continue the baseball comparison, it is a good strategy to sign the top hitter of the year at the end of the season. We should not expect him to win the batting crown next year, but we can be relatively confident of getting an above-average performance from him. There may be some regression to the mean, but a player who has the top average has above-average ability or "momentum" that makes a complete regression in one year unlikely.

The data shows that all funds that exist for 10 years do regress to a mean return of about 9%. Indeed, the data for the three-year criterion attests that momentum is lost in three years. It is very difficult to sustain top performance over a three-year period, even the top average over the period, because of changes in market sentiment, or the economy, that makes a manager's style temporarily relatively ineffective.

Buying last year's winner is often described as "chasing last year's winners" by smug professionals. Their view is that a buy-and-hold approach is better for the amateur. According to *MacLean's*, "Stock-based ("equity") funds are normally only suitable for people who intend to leave their money invested for four or five years – enough time, in most cases, to make back any losses in the event of a market turndown." (p.19, 31 Jan 00). Their reason for this dubious advice is, as we saw in the previous chapter, that they have evidence that amateur investors do poorly at timing their buying and selling. *MacLean's* gives an example of our perceived incompetence: "After two years of solid returns in 1996 and 1997, Canadian investors sank $8.1 billion into domestic stock funds in 1998 – just in time for that year's market drop. Last year [1999] investors pulled $1.3 billion out of those funds, yet the market itself was roaring back to record levels." (p.18)

This description of our folly is a bit misleading. The market did not "roar back" until late in 1999. Most of the money shifting in 1999 would have occurred earlier in the year, when the market was not "roaring back". But this brings us to the problem: how do we take advantage of trends like the surge in late 1999, and avoid the slide in the summer of 1998? *MacLean's* advice, given above, is to ignore such trends, which implies that amateurs should give up this sort of market timing. My study of the buy-last-year's-best strategy shows, I think, that we do not have to despair after all. Relying on fairly recent fund performance can give us an edge. For example, using the strategy, we would have had a gross return of 4.9% in 1998 (median return: -1.7%), and one of 51.6% in 1999 (median: 22.3%).

I should point out now that I do not use the best-of-last-year selection criterion. We can do better, in my experience, if we use shorter-term criteria, as for stocks. The main thing I wanted to show was that recent past performance is one good criterion for fund selection, as common sense leads us to believe, and contrary to what the investment establishment will tell you. Missing the best year doesn't preclude getting an above-average return from the fund the next year.

POSTSCRIPT

The preceding chapters represent an extended argument and applications for its conclusion. The conclusion is that we will do better in equity investing if we use the TrendPoint! strategy to determine when we sell our stocks. One reason for this conclusion is that this strategy gives superior returns relative to the main alternative, buy-and-hold. The only time that buy-and-hold can match or sometimes beat TrendPoint! is when the stock rises smoothly over the entire period of interest. Of course, no stock rises smoothly indefinitely, so as soon as it drops significantly TrendPoint! will become a better approach. Another reason for using TrendPoint! is that most of us are not good at ad hoc sell decisions, because of various psychological weaknesses. It is better, then, to settle this issue in advance, not by picking a sell price, but by picking an SP%. This provides for unanticipated run-ups, allowing us to stay with our stock. It also protects us if the stock "goes south" right after we buy it. TrendPoint! offers another advantage as well. Once we settle on our SP% and buy a stock there is no longer a need to monitor company news, we need only to monitor its share price. The time freed up from supervision can be used to identify new stocks that have potential, or even spent enjoying some of the money the strategy has yielded.

We can also justify relying on TrendPoint! to pick entry points, because it is a method of identifying both downward and upward trends. Once a stock comes up BP% from a bottom the time is right to buy it, providing it meets our fundamentals criteria.

If one adopts a system such as TrendPoint! one gains the ability to time trades and even the market itself. Then we can reject buy-and-hold, and all the associated stresses and disappointments. This won't guarantee that we get rich, of course. We need the co-operation of the markets for that, and some good "seed money" to get started. And using TrendPoint! won't be much help in a bear market (unless you use the short-selling version), but it will do the next-best thing: it will keep you *out* of bear markets.

BIBLIOGRAPHY

Broadfoot, James, *Investing In Emerging Growth Stocks*, Wiley, 1989.

Cassidy, Donald, *It's When You Sell That Counts* (revised edition), Irwin, 1997.

Colby, Robert & Myers, Thomas, *The Encyclopedia of Technical Market Indicators*, Irwin, 1988.

Gardner, David & Gardner, Tom, *The Motley Fool Investment Guide*, Simon & Schuster, 1996.

Gianturco, Michael, *How To Buy Technology Stocks*, Little, Brown and Company, 1996.

Graja, Christopher & Ungar, Elizabeth, *Investing In Small-Cap Stocks* (revised edition), Bloomberg, 1999.

Hagstrom, Robert, *Latticework*, Texere, 2000.

Investment Reporter, MPL Communications, Toronto.

Investor's Business Daily, *Guide To The Markets*, Wiley, 1996.

Investor's Digest of Canada, MPL Communications Inc.

Keynes, J. M., *The General Theory of Employment*, Harcourt, Brace & World, 1965.

Lassonde, Pierre, *The Gold Book*, Globe & Mail, 1996.

Loeb, Gerald, *The Battle For Investment Survival*, Fraser Publishing Co., 1988.

Lynch, Peter, *Beating The Street*, Simon & Schuster, 1994.

Malkiel, Burton, *A Random Walk Down Wall Street*, Norton, 1980.

Murphy, John J., *The Visual Investor*, Wiley, 1996.

Murphy, Michael, *Every Investor's Guide To High-Tech Stocks & Mutual Funds*, Broadway Books, 1998.

National Association of Investment Clubs (NAIC), *NAIC Official Guide*

O'Neil, William, *How To Make Money In Stocks*, 2nd ed., McGraw-Hill, 1995.

O'Shaughnessy, James, *What Works On Wall Street*, McGraw-Hill, 1997.

Radcliffe, Robert, *Investment: Concepts Analysis Strategy* (3rd edition), Harper Collins, 1990.

Schott, John W., *Mind Over Money*, Little, Brown and Company, 1998.

Siegel, Jeremy, *Stocks For The Long Run*, McGraw-Hill, 1998.

Steinberg, Jonathan, *Midas Investing*, Random House, 1996.

Stovall, Sam, *Standard & Poor's Guide To Sector Investing*, McGraw-Hill, 1995.

Zweig, Martin, *Winning On Wall Street*, Warner, 1990.

SUGGESTIONS FOR READING

Engel, Louis, *How To Buy Stocks* (8th edition), Little, Brown and Company, 1994. The most popular introduction to how stock markets and stock trading work, and probably the best. There are clones, but don't confuse this genre with books giving investment advice. It covers the "mechanics" of equity markets, an important topic not covered by the investment advice books in any detail.

Gardner, David and Gardner, Tom, *The Motley Fool Investment Guide*, Simon & Schuster, 1996. Informative and level-headed; reading this will help you benefit from the information on their big website, which is good for novice stock investors because of its instructional orientation. One of the few sites that tells you what has happened, and *why*.

Cassidy, Donald, *It's When You Sell That Counts* (revised edition), Irwin, 1997. The best book on the psychology of selling. I disagree with his "sell if you wouldn't buy now" strategy, for reasons given in Chapter Two. Every stock investor should read this.

O'Neil, William, *How To Make Money In Stocks* (2nd edition), McGraw-Hill, 1995. He presents a good system for stock picking, his CANSLIM system, and gives detailed guidance on its application.

Graja, Christopher & Ungar, Elizabeth, *Investing In Small-Cap Stocks* (revised edition), Bloomberg, 1999. The most informative book on small-cap selection. If you are going to maintain a small-cap portfolio, you ought to study this.

Investor's Business Daily, *Guide To The Markets*, Wiley, 1996. Informative and, dare I say, inspirational. Good chapter on Options, and one on how the futures market works.

Broadfoot, James, *Investing In Emerging Growth Stocks*, 1989. On small caps, but aimed more at the pros.

Gianturco, Michael, *How To Buy Technology Stocks*, Little, Brown and Company, 1995. The best guide to the high-tech sector, provides information on the main industries, and their future prospects.

Mennis, Edmund, *How The Economy Works*(2nd edition), Prentice Hall 1999. If you have no formal background in economics, this will give you enough to make sense of the economic news and the factors that influence the stock markets behind the scenes.

HIGHLY USEFUL WEBSITES

"http://www.timberleapress.com.page4.htm". Provides BP/SP% values for selected large-cap U.S. and Canadian stocks, as determined by Wayne Grennan. Using these you can calculate BP's and SP's for these stocks, as explained in *Investing: More Success With Less Stress*.

Big Charts: "http://bigcharts.marketwatch.com". Terrific Java program for interactive charting. Covers both U.S. and Canadian stocks, and even ones in foreign markets.

Yahoo!: "http://quote.yahoo.com". A top site for stock investors. Their company news seems to be more up to date than some sites. Free.

Canada Stockwatch: "http://wwwa.stockwatch.com". Offers similar Java interactive charting as Big Charts. Also features automatic email notification when a stock hits a preset high or low. Not free, but inexpensive.

Globe & Mail: "http://www.globeinvestor.com". Top site for Canadian investors, but covers U.S. stocks too. First rate mutual fund coverage. Basic site is free, but they now have a premium package called "GlobeinvestorGold" that provides extra features such as real-time quotes and advice from analysts.

National Post: "http://nationalpost.com". Contains the *Financial Post* content covering the Canadian investment scene.

Canoe: "http://www.webfin.com". Associated with the Sun newspaper chain in Canada.

Business Week. They operate an investor website in conjunction with Standard & Poor's. Premium content available for subscribers: "http://www.businessweek.com/investror/index.html"

Morningstar: U.S. "http://www.morningstar.com". Famous for their mutualfund coverage, they have one for stocks. They provide independent analyst opinions for about $100 per year.

Morningstar Canada: "http://www.morningstar.ca". Coverage for the Canadian markets comparable to their U.S. site. A separate subscription is needed.

The Motley Fool: "http://www.fool.com". Informative and educational. They provide what amounts to a course for the beginner. Their "fool" shtick gets tiresome after awhile.

Multex Investor: "http://www.marketguide.com". A big site with powerful screening tools.

"cgi.money.com/tools/retirnrate/returnrate.jsp". You can use this site to calculate rates of return. Input date of buy, amount bought, date of sell, proceeds, and a computer calculates total return and annualized return, the most useful measure of success (or failure).

INDEX

AIC Advantage Fund 108
Altamira Science & Technology 50, 101, 102
Amazon 22
Analyst ratings 78
Bonds versus stocks 2 - 4
Bonds 2 - 7
BP% 11, 32, 35, 72, 74, 78, 91, 94
Brokerage firms 80, 84, 85, 96
Buffett, Warren 23, 40, 82
Buy zone 11, 73, 78
Buy point (BP) 33, 72
Buy-and-hold 3, 5, 9, 12 - 21, 25, 31, 32, 37, 43, 73, 89, 95, 106, 111, 113, 114
C.G.I. 82
Canada Stockwatch 26-28, 91, 118
Cassidy, Donald 21, 22, 35, 117
CIBC 50, 105, 106, 107
CNBC 86, 98
Colby & Myers 11, 25-26
Commissions, trading 17, 31, 41, 110
Cyclicals 48
Demand for shares 1, 18, 22, 41-44, 52, 57, 66, 69, 72, 76, 80, 85
Diligence, due 95, 97
Dow-Jones Industrial Average 14,15
Downgrades 78
Dreman, David 54-56
E*Trade 91, 99
Earnings estimate, accuracy 52-58
Earnings per share (EPS) 52 - 59
EDGAR 96
Engel, Louis 17, 18, 117
Exchange Traded Funds (ETF's) 7, 8, 108
Fear 13, 16, 17, 34
Forward P/E 54-62, 83

Fundamentals 10-13, 22 - 24, 32, 33, 37, 38, 42, 43, 72, 75, 78, 94
Gardner, David & Tom   33, 93, 117
Garzarelli, Elaine   14
Gianturco, Michael   75, 85, 118
Globe & Mail   60, 70, 91, 97, 110
Globeinvestor.com   3, 46, 60, 70, 71, 84, 97
Gold stocks   46-48, 86, 88
Graja & Ungar   17, 38, 79, 117
Greed   13, 16, 17, 34
Guerrilla investing   8-10, 40
Health care funds   100, 105-107
Health services stocks   50
IBM   37, 78
Index funds   28, 82, 105-108
Industries   46-50, 70, 86
Internet 60, 70, 91
Investor's Business Daily   46, 64, 97
Investor's Business Daily Guide To The Markets   41, 42, 54, 117
Investor's Digest   54-56, 96, 97
IRA's   5, 18, 43
Keynes, John Maynard   14, 52
Large caps   44, 45, 51, 79, 80
Law of unexpected results   85
Loeb, Gerald   8, 9
Losses, capital   8, 21, 23, 31, 37 - 40, 104, 105, 112
Lynch, Peter   4, 6, 38, 39, 48, 52, 69, 80
MacLean's magazine   108 - 112
Malkiel, Burton   14, 87, 88
Market sentiment   16, 34, 37, 72 - 75, 86, 97, 110
Market timing   11, 12, 15, 18, 27, 112
Micro caps   44, 82
Microsoft   76 - 78
Mineral stocks   46, 47
Momentum investing   11, 22, 62 - 64, 63, 70, 71, 79, 94
Morningstar   46, 50, 60, 96, 102, 119
Moving averages   25 - 27, 73 - 75, 105

Murphy, John   24, 25
Murphy, Michael   76
National Post   97, 119
Natural resource funds   106, 48, 100
Nortel   8, 12, 18, 19, 74, 94, 107, 109
O'Neil, William   16, 23, 34, 38, 42, 46, 63, 64, 67, 68, 117
O'Shaughnessy, James   63, 70
Odd lots   16
Oil stocks   46, 48, 89
P/E expansion   43, 76 - 80
P&O Princess   83
PEG   57 - 59, 68, 69, 78, 80, 83
Portfolio management   87 - 94
Portfolio diversification   6, 9, 88 - 92, 99, 101
Price to sales ratio (P/S)   59 - 62, 69, 70, 78, 83
Price/earnings ratio (P/E), trailing   13, 22, 43, 51 - 53, 57, 59, 62 - 69, 75 - 80
Psychological weaknesses   35 - 39, 113
QQQ   7, 15
Regression to the mean   111
Regret   36, 78
Relative strength   63, 64, 70
Return, real   3, 100
Risk, systematic and unsystematic,   88 - 90
Riverstone Networks   58, 68, 84
ROB TV   86, 97, 98
Rodgers, Will   13, 33
RRSP   5, 18, 43, 50, 51, 101, 107, 108
S&P/TSE 60 index   7, 44, 107, 108
S&P 500   4, 42, 44, 46, 53, 58, 65 - 69, 88, 106, 107
Sather, Glen   93
Science & technology funds   50, 75, 100 - 107
Sector mutual funds   51, 106, 107
Sectors   46 - 51, 89, 101, 108
SEDAR   96
Short selling   16, 32

Siegel, Jeremy 2, 3, 40, 68, 73, 86
Small caps 44, 45, 50, 79 - 83
Special Situations 83
Steinberg, Jonathan 1, 23
Stock bargains 39, 65, 74, 79, 80, 85
Stock news 42, 48, 50, 51, 80, 82 - 85, 90, 91, 112, 117
Stock prices, cause of movement 33, 34, 41, 42, 47, 57, 70, 75, 77
Stop-loss price 23
Stovall, Sam 49, 89
Stress 7, 31 - 35, 104, 114
Supply of shares 41
Talvest Global Healthcare 105
Target price 22, 78
Technicians 24
Technology stocks 50, 75, 78, 88
TrendPoint! 10, 11, 15 - 19, 23 - 27, 31, 32, 40, 42, 67, 71, 75 - 78,
    88, 93, 94, 99 - 102, 104 - 107, 113
TSE 300 4, 6, 13, 28 - 31, 42, 44 - 47, 61, 82, 88, 106, 107
tulip mania 66
Upgrades 84 - 86
Value Line 83, 96
Watch list 92 - 94
Worry 31, 78
Yahoo! 50, 58 - 60, 62, 84, 97, 118
Zack's 96
Zweig, M. 35